TRADITION
METI
EQUIPMENT

A PRACTICAL TAXIDERMIST MANUAL FOR
SKINNING, STUFFING, PRESERVING, MOUNTING,
AND DISPLAYING SPECIMENS AND FURS

BY **PAUL N. HASLUCK**

ORIGINALLY PUBLISHED IN 1901

LEGACY EDITION

HASLUCK'S TRADITIONAL SKILLS LIBRARY
BOOK 2

Doublebit Press
Eugene, OR

New content, introduction, and annotations
Copyright © 2019 by Doublebit Press. All rights reserved.

Doublebit Press is an imprint of Eagle Nest Press
www.doublebitpress.com | Eugene, OR, USA

Original content under the public domain. Originally published in 1901 by Paul N. Hasluck under the title <u>Taxidermy</u>.

This title, along with other Doublebit Press books including the Hasluck's Traditional Skills Library, are available at a volume discount for youth groups, outdoors clubs, or reading groups.

Doublebit Press Legacy Edition ISBNs
Hardcover: 978-1-64389-053-1
Paperback: 978-1-64389-054-8

Disclaimer: Because of its age and historic context, this text could contain content on present-day inappropriate methods, activities, outdated medical information, unsafe chemical and mechanical processes, or culturally and racially insensitive content. Doublebit Press, or its employees, authors, and other affiliates, assume no liability for any actions performed by readers or any damages that might be related to information contained in this book. This text has been published for historical study and for personal literary enrichment toward the goal of preserving the American handcraft tradition, timeless trade skills, and traditional artisanal knowledge.

First Doublebit Press Legacy Edition Printing, 2019

Printed in the United States of America
when purchased at retail in the USA

INTRODUCTION
To The Doublebit Press Legacy Edition

The old experts of artisanal trades, country and homestead knowledge, and the woods and mountains taught timeless principles and skills for centuries. Through their timeless books, the old experts offered rich descriptions of how the world works and encouraged learning through personal experiences *by doing*. Over the last 125 years, manufacturing, farming, and construction have substantially changed. Of course, many things have gotten simpler as equipment and technology have improved. In addition, some activities of pre-digital times are now no longer in vogue, or are even outright considered inappropriate or illegal. However, despite many of the positive changes in manufacturing and crafting methods that have occurred over the years, *there are many other skills and much knowledge that have been forgotten.*

By publishing *The Hasluck Traditional Skills Library*, it is our goal at Doublebit Press to do what we can to preserve and share the works from forgotten teachers that form the cornerstone of the history of the American artisans and traditional crafts. Through remastered reprint editions of timeless classics, perhaps we can regain some of this lost knowledge for future generations.

This book is an important contribution traditional handcraft and country skills literature and has important historical and collector value toward preserving the American handcraft and outdoors tradition. The knowledge it holds is an invaluable reference for practicing skills and hand craft methods. Its chapters thoroughly discuss some of the essential building blocks of knowledge that are fundamental but may have been forgotten as equipment gets fancier and technology gets smarter. In short, this book was chosen for Legacy Edition printing because much of the basic skills and knowledge it contains has been forgotten or put to the wayside in trade for more modern conveniences and methods.

With technology playing a major role in everyday life, sometimes we need to take a step back in time to find those basic building blocks used for gaining mastery – the things that we have luckily not completely lost and has been recorded in books over the last two centuries. These skills aren't forgotten, they've just been shelved. *It's time to unshelve them once again and reclaim the lost knowledge of self-sufficiency.*

Based on this commitment to preserving our outdoors and handcraft artisanal heritage, we have taken great pride in publishing this book as a complete original work. We hope it is worthy of both study and collection by outdoors folk in the modern era of outdoors and traditional skills life.

Unlike many other photocopy reproductions of classic books that are common on the market, this Legacy Edition does not simply place poor photography of old texts on our pages and use error-prone optical scanning or computer-generated text. We want our work to speak for itself, and reflect the quality demanded by our customers who spend their hard-earned money. With this in mind, each Legacy Edition book that has been chosen for publication is carefully remastered from original print books, *with the Doublebit Legacy Edition printed and laid out in the exact way that it was presented at its original publication.* We provide a beautiful, memorable experience that is as true to the original text as best as possible, but with the aid of modern technology to make as beautiful a reading experience as possible for books that can be over a century old.

Because of its age and because it is presented in its original form, the book may contain misspellings, inking errors from print plates, and other printing blemishes that were common for the age. However, these are exactly the things that we feel give the book its character, which we preserved in this Legacy Edition. During digitization, we ensured that each illustration in the text was clean and sharp with the least amount of loss from being copied and digitized as possible. Full-page plate illustrations are presented as they were found, often including the extra blank page that was often behind a plate. For the covers, we use the original cover design to give the book its original feel. We are sure you'll appreciate the fine touches and attention to detail that your Legacy Edition has to offer.

For traditional handcrafters and classic artisanal enthusiasts who demand the best from their equipment, this Doublebit Press Legacy Edition reprint was made with you in mind. Both important and minor details have equally both been accounted for by our publishing staff, down to the cover, font, layout, and images. It is the goal of Doublebit Legacy Edition series to be worthy of collection in any outdoorsperson's library and that can be passed to future generations.

Every book selected to be in this series offers unique views and instruction on important skills, advice, tips, tidbits, anecdotes, stories, and experiences that will enrich the repertoire of any person who enjoys escaping a bit from today's modern technology-based, cookie-cutter, and highly industrialized skills. Instead, folks seeking to make things with their hands like the old days may find great value from these resurrected instructional manuals from the past. These books were not simply written to be shelved in a library – they contain our history and forgotten methods to make things with real character and energy with a *human* component.

Therefore, to learn the most basic building blocks of a craft leads to mastery of all its aspects. We hope this book helps you along this path with its rich descriptions and illustrations!

About Hasluck's Traditional Skills Library

Paul N. Hasluck was a prominent author on artisan skills and traditional handcrafts toward the end of the 19th Century. He was the editor of the magazine *Work*, which was a popular handcraft, shop skills, and artisanal craft magazine of the day. His broad expertise in making things with your hands led him to write or edit over 30 volumes on specific handcrafts, arts, and mechanics, with each manual containing invaluable information related to each craft.

Hasluck had a great eye for collecting the info that beginners and experts alike needed to perfect their craft. His volumes were loaded with helpful diagrams, tables, and illustrations that are useful even by today's digital standards. In short, Hasluck's instructional manuals were the *go-to instructional library* if someone wanted to learn a particular skill. Used by the U.S. military, the Boy and Girl Scouts, and countless folks at farms, public libraries, and homes across the world, Hasluck's instructional manuals were the perfect handy book" for learning.

This Doublebit Press Legacy Edition republishes this tradition of handcrafted quality and artisanal work. We hope that this deluxe printed edition of this work will help you gain mastery in your craft, as it is presented in the exact form that it was originally published. Even today, the knowledge contained within its pages are timeless and have much to teach!

Finally, as art, Hasluck's manuals contain beautiful illustrations and line art that are a sign of simpler, yet authentic times when quality mattered and craftsmanship was king. This collectible volume makes a great addition to the bookshelf of any handcrafter, maker, artisan, farmer, homesteader, or outdoors enthusiast!

TAXIDERMY

COMPRISING THE SKINNING, STUFFING, AND
MOUNTING OF BIRDS, MAMMALS,
AND FISH

WITH NUMEROUS ENGRAVINGS AND DIAGRAMS

EDITED BY

PAUL N. HASLUCK

EDITOR OF "WORK" AND "BUILDING WORLD,"
AUTHOR OF "HANDYBOOKS FOR HANDICRAFTS," ETC. ETC.

CASSELL AND COMPANY, Limited
LONDON, PARIS, NEW YORK & MELBOURNE
1901

ALL RIGHTS RESERVED

PREFACE.

This Handbook contains, in a form convenient for everyday use, a comprehensive digest of the knowledge of Taxidermy, scattered over nearly twenty thousand columns of Work—one of the weekly journals it is my fortune to edit—and supplies concise information on the general principles of the subjects on which it treats.

In preparing for publication in book form the mass of relevant matter contained in the volumes of Work, some of it necessarily had to be re-arranged and partly re-written. However, the principal contents of this handbook consist substantially of illustrated articles by Mr. J. Fielding-Cottrill originally contributed to Work.

Readers who may desire additional information respecting special details of the matters dealt with in this Handbook, or instructions on kindred subjects, should address a question to Work, so that it may be answered in the columns of that journal.

P. N. HASLUCK.

La Belle Sauvage, London,
    April, 1901.

CONTENTS.

CHAP.	PAGE
I.—Skinning Birds	9
II.—Stuffing and Mounting Birds	24
III.—Skinning and Stuffing Mammals . . .	48
IV.—Animals' Horned Heads: Polishing and Mounting Horns	68
V.—Skinning, Stuffing, and Casting Fish . .	94
VI.—Preserving, Cleaning, and Dyeing Skins . .	107
VII.—Preserving Insects and Birds' Eggs . . .	132
VIII.—Cases for Stuffed Specimens	149
Index	157

LIST OF ILLUSTRATIONS.

FIG.		PAGE
1.	Skinning Knife	10
2.	Scissors	10
3.	Round-nose Pliers	11
4.	Cutting Nippers	12
5.	Side Cutters	12
6.	Side Cutters	12
7.	Flat-nose Pliers	12
8.	Bellhanger's Pliers	12
9.	Brain-spoon and Hook	13
10.	Feather Pliers	13
11.	Stuffing-iron	14
12.	Stuffing-iron	14
13.	Bodkin	14
14.	Suspending Hook	15
15.	Chain and Hooks	15
16.	Diagram of Bird	19
17.	Modelled Body for Bird	26
18.	Method of Sewing Up Bird	28
19.	Method of Bolting Leg Wire	29
20.	Bird Bound with Threads	30
21.	Bird Bound with Threads	31
22.	Bird, Braced and Bound	32
23.	Wiring for Soft Body of Bird	33
24.	Cork Foundation for Body of Bird	35
25.	Artificial Eyes	37
26.	Bird's Wings Spread Out	42
27.	Section of Bird's Head on Screen	43
28.	Handle for Bird Screen	45
29.	Diagram of Screen	46
30.	Diagram of Screen	46
31.	Turned Base for Screen	46
32.	Screen with Stuffed Bird	47
33.	Measurement of Waterbuck	49
34.	Squirrel	51
35.	Hand of Monkey	57
36.	Bones of Animal's Hind Leg	60
37.	Artificial Hind Leg	61
38.	Body for Mammal	63
39.	Wiring for Loose Stuffing of Mammal	64
40.	Wiring for Loose Stuffing of Mammal	65
41.	Veined Artificial Eye	66
42.	Veined and Cornered Artificial Eye	66
43.	Moleskin Purse	67
44.	Back of Horned Head	69
45.	Turned Wood for Ear Block	73
46.	Turned Wood for Ear Block	73
47.	Skull with Centre Board for Modelled Neck	74
48.	Skull with Centre Board for Loose Neck	75
49.	Neck Board for Horned Head	76
50.	Plaster Head with Tow Neck	77
51.	Skin Nailed on Neck Board	79
52.	Ear, Blocked and Bound	80
53.	Ear, Blocked and Bound	80
54.	Finished Horned Head	81
55.	Shield Mount, showing Position of Neck Board	82
56.	Shield Mount	82
57.	Shield Mount	82
58.	Shield Mount	83
59.	Shield Mount	83
60.	Shield Mount	83
61.	Oval Mount	83
62.	Mounting Stag's Antlers	84
63.	Mounting Stag's Antlers	84
64.	Mounting Stag's Antlers	84
65.	Front View of Elephant Tusk Mount	86
66.	Side View of Elephant Tusk Mount	87
67.	Perch Ready for Opening	95

FIG.	PAGE
68.—Wire Shape of Fish	95
69.—Fish embedded in Clay	102
70.—Clay-embedded Fish covered with Plaster	103
71.—Section of Plaster Fish-mould	104
72.—Plaster Cast of Fish	105
73.—Skin-stretching Frame	108
74.—Corner of Skin-stretching Frame	108
75.—Shave-hook for Dressing Skins	109
76.—Serrated Blade of Shave-hook	100
77.—Furrier's Double-edged Knife	110
78.—Furrier's Single-edged Knife	110
79.—Furrier's Horse or Beam	111
80.—Sandpaper Block for Rubbing Skins	111
81, 82.—Insect Envelope	133
83.—Section of Setting Board	135
84.—Butterfly on Setting Board	135
85.—Single Book Box for Insects	139
86.—Half of Double Book Box for Insects	139
87.—Double Book Box for Insects	140
88.—Cork Lining of Insect Cabinet	140
89.—Drawers with Hinged Pillar	141
90.—Body of Cabinet	144
91.—Drawer Section showing Groove and Runner	144
92.—Drawer with Grooved Side	145
93, 94.—Drawer Sections showing Grooves and Runners	145
95.—Screw to Prevent Drawers Coming Out	146
96–100.—Fixing Glass in Drawers	146
101.—Fixing Glass in Drawers	147
102.—Partitions for Egg Cabinet	147
103.—Joint for Box Case	150
104.—Section of Case Upright	150
105.—Section of Bamboo Case Upright	150
106.—Canted Corner Case	151
107, 108.—Sections of Fish Cases having Bent Glass Fronts	152

TAXIDERMY.

CHAPTER I.

SKINNING BIRDS.

TAXIDERMY has been defined as the art of preparing and preserving the skins of animals, and also of stuffing and mounting them so as to impart to them as close a resemblance to the living forms as possible. The art is classified easily into three broad divisions: (1) Birds, (2) Mammals, (3) Fish; and, as may be seen by a glance through the following pages, this classification is adhered to in this book. Also, taxidermy has been extended further so as to include the preserving and setting of insects, a subject really forming part of the science of entomology; brief instructions in this minor branch of taxidermy are given, however, in order to make this handbook complete. The skinning, stuffing, and mounting of birds is the first part of the subject to receive treatment.

Very few tools are required by the taxidermist, it being possible to skin both birds and small mammals with only a penknife and a pair of scissors, and with the further aid of a pair of pliers to stuff and set them up.

It is not, however, always well to work with makeshift tools, and most, if not all, of the following should be obtained; but beginners are advised not to purchase the "boxes of bird-stuffing tools," as advertised, or they may find half of the tools useless and the other half unnecessary.

The first indispensable article is a knife (Fig. 1). A penknife, if it is capable of holding a good edge, will answer just as well as a case of lancets and scalpels. A good knife for the purpose is an old "skiving" knife, used by shoemakers, and this may be kept keen on a strop covered with two different grades of emery-cloth; or an oilstone may be used instead of the strop.

Fig. 1.—Skinning Knife.   Fig. 2.—Scissors.

The next tool required is a pair of fine-pointed scissors (Fig. 2) of the kind known as "grape scissors," which are used for thinning grapes; they have long handles and short, straight, fine blades. It is advisable, but not essential, to have a second and stronger pair with blunt ends for cutting up tow, and they should be large and strong.

Round-nose pliers (Fig. 3) are mainly used for fine wire, so the finer they are the better. Cutting nippers (Fig. 4) should be large and strong, as they are for use in cutting wire; they can have the cutting planes either in front or at the sides. Side cutters (Figs. 5 and 6), also, are useful; they are the kind used for opening champagne or soda-water

Fig. 3.—Round-nose Pliers.

bottles. They are similar in shape to the ordinary nail nippers, but they have the jaws straight instead of being curved. These are not used generally by taxidermists, but they are almost invaluable, serving as bone forceps for cutting legs, wings, etc., and they will cut a muscle as well as will scissors, besides being very useful for fine wires. Flat-nose pliers (Fig. 7) are useful for heavier wires. Many use the common shape of bellhanger's pliers (Fig. 8), as these combine the cutting and the flat-nosed pliers.

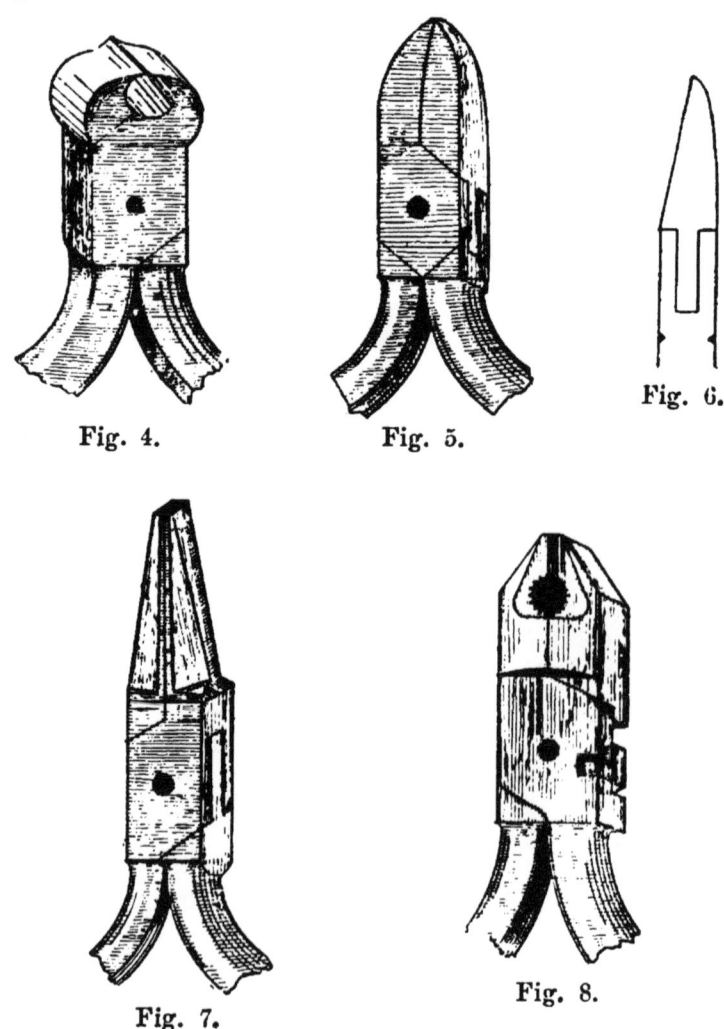

Fig. 4. Fig. 5. Fig. 6.

Fig. 7. Fig. 8.

Fig. 4, Cutting Nippers; Figs. 5 and 6, Side Cutters; Fig. 7, Flat-nose Pliers; Fig. 8, Bellhanger's Pliers.

The brain-spoon and hook are used by some, but are not really necessary. To make a useful tool, file a knitting needle into a gradually tapering point, and while hot turn it into a small hook as shown in Fig. 9. Hammer the other end into the approximate shape of a spoon, and then trim it up with a file.

An appliance is required with which to put the feathers straight, and for this purpose some use a

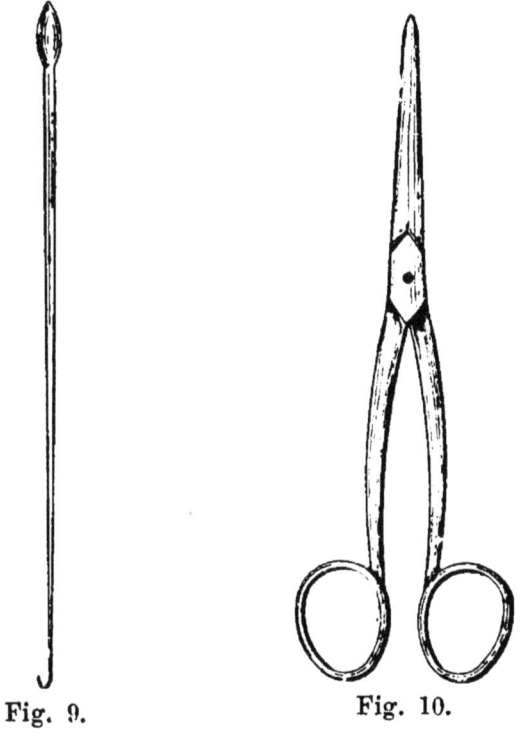

Fig. 9.
Brain-spoon and Hook.

Fig. 10.
Feather Pliers.

pair of watchmaker's pliers with rather long jaws. But very little strength is necessary, so they may be as fine as possible, and have rather broad "noses." Scissor pliers (Fig. 10) seem to be a perfect tool for the purpose when the bars at the end of both jaws have been filed down. Next best to the scissor pliers are straight or curved tweezers, 6 in. to 8 in. long.

The stuffing-iron is shown by Figs. 11 and 12; to make it, hammer one end of a steel knitting needle flat like a chisel, and file one or two nicks in the flattened part; then fit it into a handle.

Two shoemaker's awls should be obtained, one

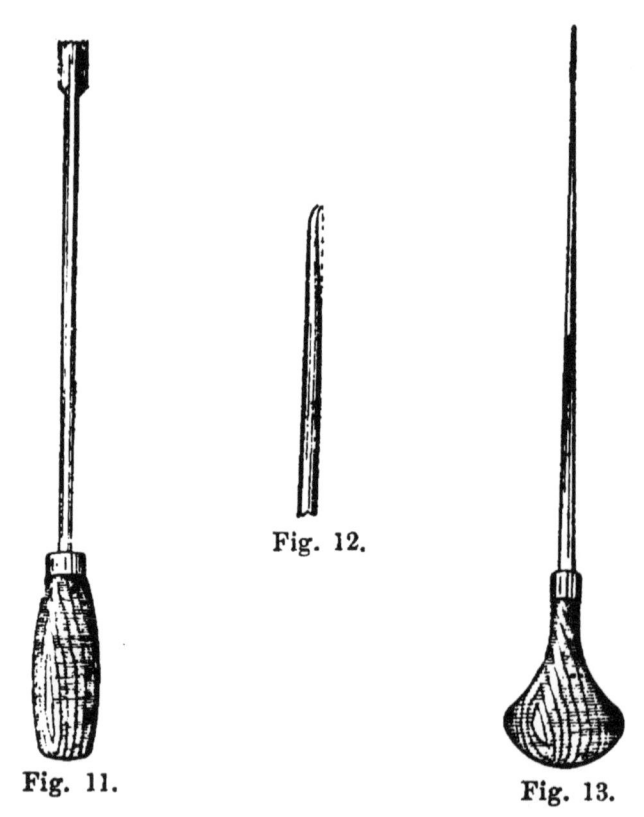

Fig. 12.

Fig. 11.　　　　　　　　　　　Fig. 13.

Figs. 11 and 12, Stuffing-iron; Fig. 13, Bodkin.

fine and the other large; they will come in for a lot of useful work. One or two knitting needles will be found useful.

A bodkin inserted into a handle is also useful; it can be made from a knitting needle, one end of which is sharpened to a fine tapering point, the other being put into a handle (see Fig. 13). A three-

SKINNING BIRDS.

cornered file for sharpening the wires is also required.

A small sharp hook is fastened to a cord suspended from a hook fixed in the ceiling. On this hook (Fig. 14) the bird is hung whilst being skinned, and thus the left hand of the operator is at liberty to keep the feathers away from the flesh. Some use instead a chain and hooks, as shown by Fig. 15.

With the tools enumerated above any bird can be

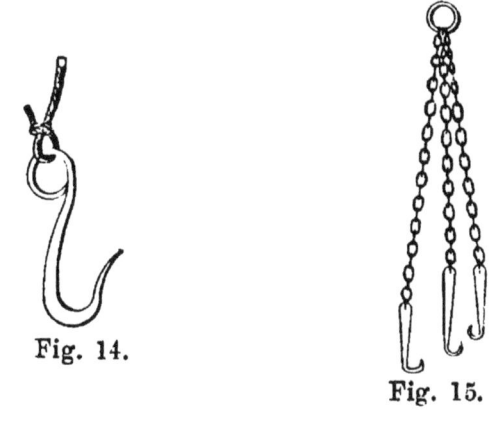

Fig. 14.

Fig. 15.

Fig. 14, Suspending Hook; Fig. 15, Chain and Hooks.

stuffed, or, with the addition of a large stuffing-iron, any animal—at least up to a wolf, and but few beginners will venture beyond this. Other requisites are a packet of pins, a reel of cotton, a needle (the ordinary kind will do, though many use the triangular-pointed glover's needle), some tow, a little cotton-wool, and some plaster-of-paris. This plaster is extremely useful, and should always be within reach. Instead of tow, a kind of fine shaving, known as wood-wool, is coming into use as a stuffing material.

The taxidermist will require some kind of preservative. Those mentioned below are considered specially suitable for birds, but in a later chapter some additional recipes may be given for use in stuffing mammals.

The preservative is put on to dry the skins, and during this drying the fibres naturally contract, drawing up the skin in every direction. To counteract this, it is usual to place inside the skin a false body of tow or wool.

The preservative used by most taxidermists is the arsenical soap invented by Becœur in 1770, or a modification of it. Its composition is camphor, 5 oz.; white arsenic, 2 lb.; white soap, 2 lb.; salts of tartar, 2 oz.; chalk, 4 oz. Several modifications of this soap used by some taxidermists are given below:—

(1) Corrosive sublimate, $\frac{1}{2}$ oz.; arsenic, $\frac{1}{2}$ oz.; spirit of wine, 4 drams; camphor, $\frac{1}{2}$ oz.; white soap, 6 oz.

(2) Arsenic, 1 oz.; white soap, 1 oz.; carbonate potash, 1 dram; water, 6 drams; camphor, 2 drams.

(3) White soap, 4 lb.; arsenic, 1 lb.; camphor, 1 oz.

Most taxidermists have their own special recipe, but the above are sufficient to show the proportions in general use.

Preservatives are made something after this manner. The soap is cut up into a vessel containing water placed over or near a fire and left to dissolve. When cooked, and while still hot, the arsenic—in all cases in the form of powder—is gradually stirred in, as are the chalk, tartar, sublimate, etc. Do not hold the head over the pan, because disagreeable fumes are given off. The camphor, in all cases, is best dissolved in spirit of wine separately and added to the cooling, but not yet cold, mixture, stirring briskly all the time. Label the mixture "DEADLY POISON," and be careful in using it. It should be of the same consistency as thick dairy cream, and a small brush should be kept solely for use with it. If too dry, dilute it with warm water. Arsenical soap is good in its way, but is very dangerous to use, and the taxidermist cannot be too careful with it. Do not be persuaded to use a powder compounded with arsenic, or injury to the skin of the hands will result.

Browne's non-poisonous preservative is perhaps the most popular preserving soap, and consists of whiting 1½ lb., white curd soap ½ lb.; chloride of lime ½ oz., tincture of musk ½ oz., and water 1 pt. To prepare it, cut the soap into thin pieces, and boil it with the whiting and water. The boiling is simply to dissolve the soap, and when that is done, and the whiting mixed in, it should be removed from the fire. The longer it is boiled, the more water is required. When it attains the consistence of thick cream, take it off the fire, and stir in the chloride, but keep the head away, because of the disagreeable fumes which arise. When cold, add the musk, which is used mainly to hide the objectionable smell. Tincture of musk can be replaced by tincture of camphor, made by dissolving camphor in spirit of wine, though it is much less permanent. Be careful to add the tincture to the mixture when cold, or much of its strength will be lost. The mixture is perhaps easier made by slightly increasing the amount of water, though it is better to make it thick and then for use thin it with methylated spirit. If placed in small jars, securely fastened down, this preservative will keep for an indefinite time. Of course, if it gets too dry it may be diluted with water. It is superior to any of the arsenical soaps, and is cheap, non-poisonous, and has a pleasant smell. So cheap is it, that it works out at less than a farthing for a starling or blackbird; by using the tincture of camphor instead of musk it is a little cheaper but not so good. This preservative is painted on the inside of the skins, then the "stuffing" is done; thus the preservative is left on for all time. Of course, the pre-

B

servative applies to the skin alone, the hair or feathers not requiring such treatment.

Having the tools, plaster-of-paris, tow, cotton-wool, needle and cotton, preservative, etc., within reach of the hands, a beginning can be made at skinning the bird, which by preference should be a starling, because it is of medium size and its skin is tough.

Spread a piece of paper upon the table and upon this place the bird, with its head pointing towards the operator. See that the mouth is well filled with wadding to prevent anything running out and staining the feathers. Then pass a needle and cotton through the nostrils and tie the mandibles together; this is very important with white-fronted birds, and also with woodpeckers; but, though not quite so imperative with a starling, it had better be done in all cases.

Now break the bones of the wing as close to the body as possible (see Fig. 16, D D). In cases where the fingers or pliers are not able to do this, the wing should be struck a smart blow with a piece of wood (a round heavy ruler will do), the bird being held with the wing resting against the edge of the table. With the fingers and the point of the knife carefully separate the feathers along the breast, leaving the skin bare. Cut the skin along the full length of the breast, cutting towards the tail, as shown at A B (Fig. 16). Having done this, carefully lift up one side of the shining edges of the skin and proceed to separate the skin from the flesh by pushing, cutting, or anything but *pulling*, and in doing this keep the edge of the knife upon the flesh. Take time over this or the skin may easily be stretched out of all proportion. Continually sprinkle plaster-of-paris upon the bare flesh to prevent the feathers getting soiled, and frequently dip the fingers in the powdered plaster for the same purpose. Having gone as far as possible on the one side, turn and repeat with the other. With a little care the neck may now be exposed, and with the aid of the side cutters (Fig. 5, p. 12), it must be cut off as near the body as possible, as shown at C, Fig. 16. Use plenty of plaster now. The cutting away of the neck considerably frees the shoulders, and it will now, no doubt, be possible to work to the wing sufficiently to cut it off (see D D). Here, again, the side cutters can be used; in fact, no difficulty will be met with in cutting through the

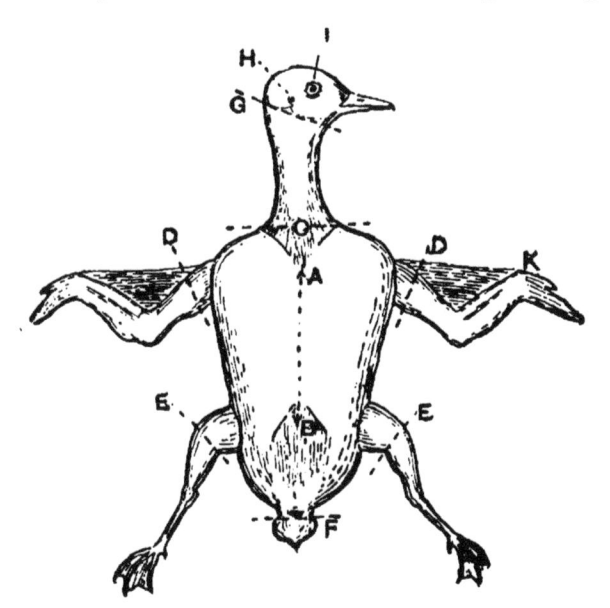

Fig. 16.—Diagram of Bird.

largest bird's wing with them, though in the present case the scissors will be quite sufficient. Cut off the other wing, and suspend the bird by the hanging-hook (Fig. 14, p. 15). With great care release the skin from the back, using the left hand to keep the feathers away from the flesh. Sprinkle on plenty of plaster. The legs will soon be reached. Seize the foot with the right hand and push upwards, at the same time pushing the skin down with the left hand. Daylight is now seen between the flesh and the skin. Slip in the scissors and cut the leg at the joint (see E E, Fig. 16). Repeat with the other leg and proceed with the skinning, but be careful, as the skin along the back is very thin. The two oval-shaped bodies seen presently are the oil glands on the tail (the "parson's nose" known to the cook). The bone should be carefully cut through with the side cutters or scissors (see F, Fig. 16). Skin upwards, instead of downwards, as the corner is being turned now to get to the vent. Careful work here will quickly leave the skin hanging by the lower part of the bowel, which, being cut through with the scissors, releases the whole skin.

Take the body off the hook, but do not throw it away yet. Then fasten the hook into the neck, and, with the fingers only, proceed to ease, not by any means pull the skin from the neck. A little care is wanted when the head is reached. Still the skin slides off easily until a whitish piece of skin appears on each side (H, Fig. 16). These pieces are the ears, and the skin must come out entirely. This is much easier done by putting the awl under and lifting up; take care that the awl goes under the bottom skin. If done properly, the skin of the ear will stand out like a little pocket until the air is pressed out of it. Now carefully work on until progress is stopped again by a darker part on each side. These are the eyes (I, Fig. 16), and with the knife cut towards the flesh very gently. An almost transparent skin near the eye now is cut through, and the skin is found to hang only by the corner nearest the beak. Now cut off the neck at the base of the skull (G, Fig. 16). Lay down the skin, take out the wadding from the mouth, and lift out each eye with the awl. Next remove the tongue by placing the knife under it and the thumb over it, then pull steadily. Now enlarge the opening at the back of the skull, cutting more towards the mouth; in fact, none of the top of the skull should be removed. Now, with the point of the knife or the brain-spoon, scoop out the brains. Then carefully scrape and cut away all the little pieces of flesh which will be found at the bottom of the orbits and along the sides of the head.

The legs and wings now require cleaning and freeing from flesh. It is immaterial which are done first. The skin of the legs is easily turned back to as far as the feathers go, and, by cutting the tendons at the "knee" joint, the whole of the flesh may be removed in one piece. Now paint the bone and the skin with preservative. Wrap some fine tow round the bone till it is about equal to the real leg, and then draw the skin back. Repeat on the other side. To clear the tail it is necessary to take away the oil glands, but much care will be required to prevent cutting the tail feathers, in which case they will fall out and cannot be replaced.

Now turn to the wings. By holding the bone in one hand the joint is soon reached, and no difficulty is found in passing this joint. Here there are two bones enclosing a small oval piece of flesh. As the wing feathers are attached to the larger of these bones, it cannot well be skinned, so the flesh is removed by using the point of the knife and cutting away the flesh in little pieces. In larger birds the wing is opened on the underside, all flesh removed, well painted with preservative, the space refilled with tow, and then neatly sewn up. Tie a piece of thread through this opening to the larger bone, and leave one end long. Then repeat with the other wing.

Any lines of fat on the skin are now removed by scraping, not cutting. The head, its skin, and the skin of the neck are well anointed with preservative, the skull filled with cut tow, the orbits with cotton-wool, and the skin turned back again. This is rather difficult to describe, as well as to perform. A certain amount of knack is necessary in this. Place the thumb at the back of the skull and push, at the same time drawing the skin over by a kind of scratching motion. When once it starts to slide, all will go right. Anoint the wing-bones and the skin with preservative and pull them right. Do the same with the tail. By this time the whole skin is right side out, and the head, neck, wings, legs, and tail have been covered with preservative, but the body part has been neglected; therefore, carefully paint all this part, the left hand keeping the feathers from being injured. Put right the feathers on the head by using the knitting needle; place this in the eye, carefully pass it between the skin and the skull, and gently draw it along the inside of the skin of the head, etc., scratching it, as it were, with the end.

The wings must now be tied together by the threads which were left for this purpose. Measure the distance across the back of the real body, and leave the wings that distance only apart.

Many taxidermists work upwards instead of downwards. They cut an opening from the breast to the vent, release the legs, then the tail, and work round to the wings. A free course is thus gained to the skull, where the separating cut is made, leaving the body and neck in one piece.

Many white-fronted birds are quite spoilt by being opened down the breast, for sooner or later the fat is drawn from the interior by capillary attraction through the thread used in sewing up, and makes its presence shown by an ugly line of rusty brown, lying in relief against the snow-white feathers of the breast. Even after removing, with much care, patience, and trouble, the disfiguring line it will reappear over and over again, and it is hopeless to try to prevent it. For this reason white birds should be opened on the back, where there are plenty of feathers to conceal the cut, and the breast will be left uninjured. Make a cut from the neck to above the legs. Separate the wings and then the neck. Now hang the bird by the hook and continue to the legs; separate at the tail. Be careful over the breast, as if the skin is stretched at all the feathers will separate in a straight line, forming a very disfiguring parting. Another method is to skin from under the wing, a cut being made reaching from under the wing to over the leg. The wing is separated, and the bird is suspended and finished as usual.

Some birds have heads larger than their necks, the skin refusing to pass over the head. Among these are ducks, geese, swans, some grebes, and woodpeckers. With these skin as far up the neck as possible, cut off the neck, and turn the skin right side out. Cut the skin on the side of the face to about as far as the remnant of the neck. The skull is next skinned through this opening, cleaned, anointed with preservative, stuffed, and returned. When carefully sewn up, a cursory glance should not ascertain that the side has been touched. If the bird is crested, the cut may well be made by the side of the crest.

In skinning owls, take great care with the head and tail. The skin is little thicker than tissue paper, and any carelessness might cause injury. There are many little points to be observed in the skinning and mounting of owls. For instance, the orifices of the ears are very large, and if they be skinned some difficulty will be found in disposing of this skin. If the skinning be continued to the beak, the character of the face will be lost. The best plan is to skin up to the ears, and leave this part alone as it is; then skin on the top of the head and the eye. With the largest awl, lift out the eye between the bone and the skin. If this is not understood, the tongue and the greater part of the bottom of the skull (forming the palate) may be cut out, the brain removed, and the eyes taken out from this position with ease. The full expression is left, and owls skinned in this way will be very lifelike. A dirty and inferior plan is to skin down to the beak and gouge out the contents of the eye, leaving the cup of the eye still in its place.

CHAPTER II.

STUFFING AND MOUNTING BIRDS.

IF a bird skin has been kept unstuffed for a long while, it will have become stiff, and must be softened or relaxed before stuffing should be attempted. For this purpose, a relaxing box is necessary. This is a wooden box with a tightly-fitting cover, the whole of the inside of which has been covered to the depth of 1 in. or 2 in. with plaster-of-paris mixed in the usual way with water. This plaster, when dry, adheres to the wood. Water is poured into the box and allowed to stay until the plaster has absorbed as much as it can. The rest is poured away, and the box is ready for use. Place the skin in the box and allow to remain until the feet and wings can be opened and closed. The time varies with the size of the birds, humming-birds taking a day or less, while the eagle may require four days or more. All the stuffing must be removed and the inside of the skin well scraped to stretch the fibres; the legs of some birds require a drill, needle, or pricker forced up to make a passage for the supporting wires. Everything must be in readiness before the skin is taken from the box, and the work finished without delay, as relaxed skins dry quickly. In place of the relaxing box an earthen pan half filled with damp sand may be used. Wrap each skin in a clean rag and place it on the damp sand; then cover with more damp sand, cover the whole with a damp cloth, and place in a shady place. In the course of, say, two or three days remove the top sand and examine the skins. If the feet and wings can be spread out by gently working them, they are ready for stuffing; if not, the skins are again covered and placed away for another day or two. Practical taxidermists frequently pour warm water into the skin, or sometimes immerse the whole of the skin in water, covering the feathers afterwards with plaster. The skins of both birds and squirrels are certainly much easier and better mounted fresh. Relaxed skins dry very quickly, and many have a wooden and unnatural appearance when stuffed.

There are many ways of stuffing birds, and many ways of wiring them. Waterton perfected a neat but troublesome method of setting up birds without using wires, but this is hardly a practical method. A good working method consists in modelling a firm body of tow. A piece of wire about twice as long as the bird has one end filed to a sharp point; if for a large bird it is left with a bayonet-shaped or triangular point, so that each edge will cut. The other end may or may not be pointed. Now commence at about 1 in. from the blunt end to wrap some tow round it until it approaches in size to the real body. This end of the wire must now be hooked and turned back into the tow; then by pulling at the other end, it will be firmly locked (see Fig. 17). Measure carefully in every direction, binding on more tow with cotton where wanted, and if there are any hollows difficult to be formed a long darning needle may be used to sew through and through. Continue this binding on and stitching through till the body is an exact facsimile of the original. Practically this takes but a few minutes to do. The only variation which can be allowed is that the artificial body may be a shade smaller than the real one, for then it is easy by means of the stuffing-iron to stuff in more tow, cut up into small pieces. If, however, it be only a little larger the result will be anything but pleasing. If the breast be too wide the feathers will never sit right, and in many birds an ugly parting will be shown all down the breast, while the wings will not lie properly. Having done this, two wires, at least a size larger than the body wire, and about twice as long as the leg, must be cut. These require pointing with the file, and are then to be entered in at the ball of the foot and gradually pushed up. Be careful how the "knee" joint (really the heel) is passed; push it on through the artificial leg already

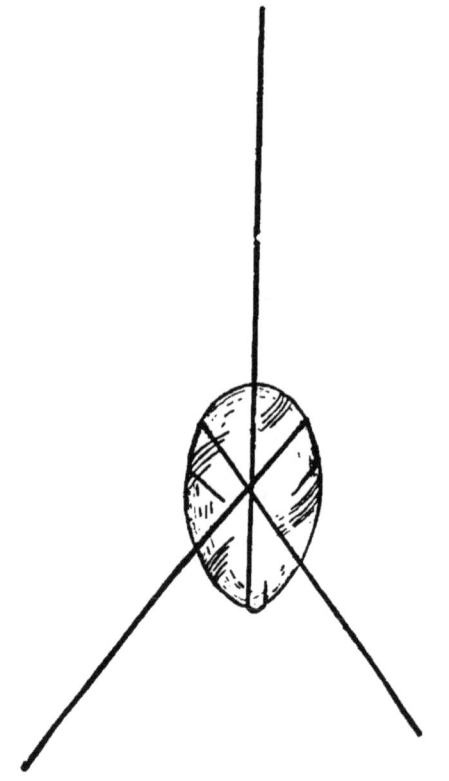

Fig. 17.—Modelled Body for Bird.

made. Repeat with the other leg. In practice, it will be found better to leave this artificial leg until the wire is in, and then wrap the tow round both wire and bone.

The wings are already tied together at the original distance, and nothing more is required here. The head, too, is already stuffed with tow, and the orbits with cotton-wool; but be careful that the cotton-wool is confined to the orbits, for, though a pointed wire will readily pass through tow, if only a little cotton-wool be present the wire will not pass.

Now gently pass some pieces of tow up the neck, using the feather pliers (Fig. 10, p. 13), making sure that they rest well against the base of the skull; one piece may be forced into the skull and another into the mouth, so that they form a connection between the head and neck. The only thing to guard against here is making the neck too long. In some positions the artificial neck is almost absent. Take the artificial body in the hands, and gently force the pointed wire up the neck and through the skull, allowing the point to come out of the centre, level with the middle of the eyes, but rather further back. Now gradually pull the skin over, using more persuasion than force. It may, perhaps, make matters somewhat easier if the neck wire be bent at right angles before putting the artificial body into the skin, and then to straighten it again.

Having placed the body in nicely, the next thing is bolting the leg wires. To do this, the foot must be taken in the left hand and lifted up. Then the wire is taken in the right hand and forced through the body for some distance, the skin being pushed downwards out of the way. With the round-nose pliers (Fig. 3, p. 11) the pointed end is bent at right angles, and then bent again so that the point enters the body. A strong, steady pull is now given to this wire, the body being held firmly with the left hand, until the whole of the returning piece is fixed tightly. A reference to Fig. 17, p. 26, should make this clear. Now lift up the bird by this leg and see if all is firm. There should not be the slightest sign of a shake. Nothing more must be done until this is quite firm. Now attend to the other leg, and again test it. Lift up the skin into place again, and proceed with the finishing. The legs must be bent downwards and forwards. In many stuffed birds it will be seen that the legs are too far back. This is a very great, but a very common, fault. The opposite fault, having the legs too far forward, is very rarely seen, and beginners will do well to aim for it at first. The body should be closely examined to see if any improvements can be made. If any part is too full, probably pressing with the fingers will

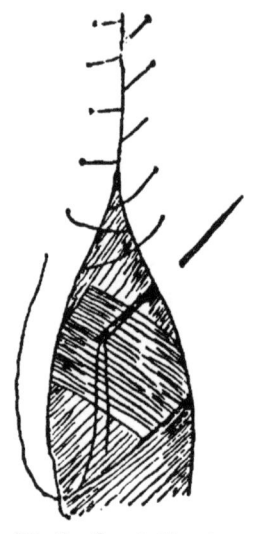

Fig. 18.—Method of Sewing Up Bird.

put matters right; if any part is not full enough, a piece of cut tow must be put in, and pushed into place with the stuffing-iron. Notice these three points: (a) that the back is nicely sloped; (b) that the breast is well filled and rounded; (c) that between the legs is narrow.

All being satisfactory, the skin must be sewn up by an under and over stitch (Fig. 18), drawn tightly after every two or three stitches. Take care that feathers are not caught in. Now the eyes (see p. 36) can be put in, though perhaps it is preferable to do this directly the head is stuffed. Others finish the body without the eyes, and put them in when the bird is dry.

The method of inserting the artificial eye is first to put a small quantity of putty into the orbit and then put in the eye, which should not be nearly as large as the real eye, but just a shade larger than the iris. Now with a needle gently pull the lid over, and do not leave it till it is perfectly round. Guard,

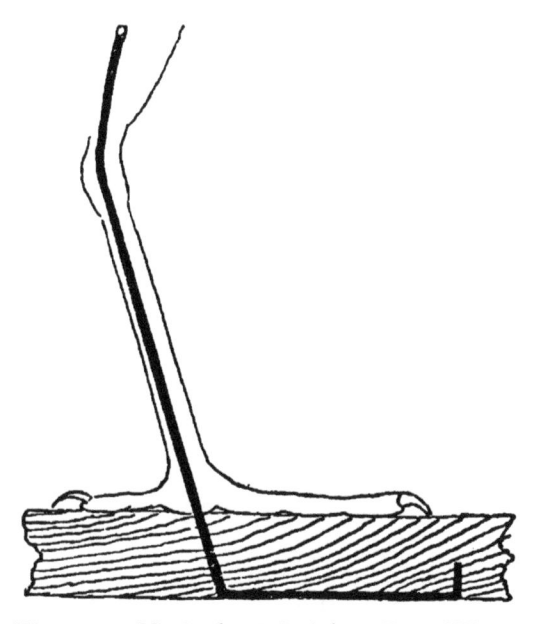

Fig. 19.—Method of Bolting Leg Wire.

also, against leaving them too staring. Dealers in taxidermists' requisites supply a gross of artificial eyes, assorted, for a few shillings.

Birds with white or light feathers may be stained if putty is used in them, so this may be replaced by pipeclay. Some do not use anything, but this is not a wise course. Cut off the head wire, leaving a small piece still projecting from the skull. As one end of this wire is pointed, it comes in well to support the tail. Push it through the butt of the tail firmly into the body so that there will be no fear of its giving way.

Birds that have wattles will require these fleshy lobes to be produced artificially, as the wattles will be found to have shrunk to mere scraps of skin. They are treated so that the original shape and colour is restored, by adding an external composition— wax or, better, papier-mâché. Apply the wax when hot with a brush, or the papier-mâché with the fingers and a penknife. Model with awls and the

Fig. 20.—Bird Bound with Threads.

knife (failing modelling tools), and then colour. Wattles vary in colour, but usually are of some bright tint, such as red, blue, or yellow.

The bird is now ready for fixing to its stand. The leg wires must go quite through and be firmly bolted in (see Fig. 19). Of course, if fixed on a temporary branch or perch, they will not be so bolted, but can be made sufficiently secure by slightly twisting the wire. Bend the head downwards and then upwards to imitate nature, and the bird will look rather more lifelike. The wings now drop, and they should be lifted up into their places and pinned into position by one or more pins or pointed wires. Now, with the feather pliers, every feather must very carefully be coaxed into place, using only a very gentle hand indeed, though many use a camel-hair mop or brush to assist in this work, which will require much patience. After all, probably a few feathers will persist in rising, and these must be bound down, and whatever position is given to them when wet will be retained when dry. Several pins or wires are

Fig. 21.—Bird Bound with Threads.

standing part of their distance out of the wings. Another pin or two should be put into the middle of the back and another into the breast, and then, starting from one of these, that on the back for preference, a piece of cotton or wool is wound in a zigzag fashion from one to the other, pressing rather heavier where the feathers rise, and lighter where all appears right (see Fig. 20). Probably some regular method of proceeding will be preferred, so make it a rule to bind down the back first, then the breast, etc., or begin at the head and gradually wind the cotton down the neck and round the body (see Fig. 21). Tapes or strips of paper may be used instead of the cotton. No two taxidermists work exactly the same, and one man rarely binds two birds alike, because it is not always the same feathers which require this treatment, although the upper wing-coverts will generally be found the troublesome ones.

If the tail was not attended to before the bird was bound, it must now be seen to. A fine entomological pin (see p. 136) may be forced through the quills of the tail feathers, and the feathers may be spread or closed upon this pin as desired. A simpler

Fig. 22.—Bird Braced and Bound.

and commoner plan is to spread the tail as desired, and then pin the feathers between slips of thin card. When dry the paper or card can be removed, and the feathers will retain their position (see Figs. 20, 21, and 22). This latter method is largely used upon the wings, when they are raised or extended, as in Fig 22. Now cut off the head wire close to the head, for if left till the bird is dry the feathers will be permanently ruffled.

Another plan of making a body is sometimes known as the soft body process. In this case a loop is formed about two-thirds down the body wire, both ends of which are pointed. The longer end is pushed up into the neck and out of the skull, so that the other end can enter the body, and then the

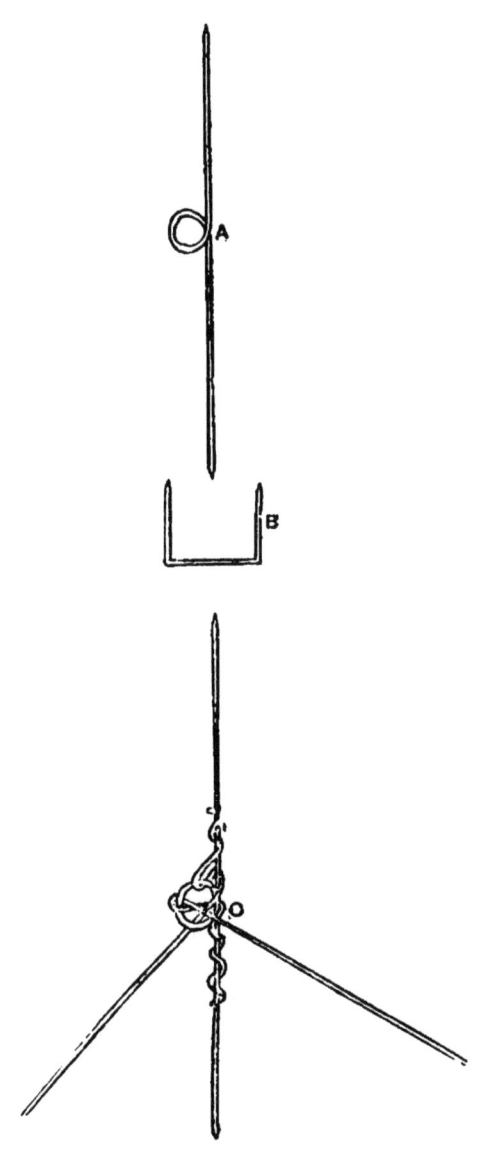

Fig. 23.—Wiring for Soft Body of Bird.

whole is pulled backwards till the shorter end goes into the tail, leaving the loop in the middle of the body, where it lies upon a piece of tow reaching from the neck to the tail. Two other pointed wires are pushed up the legs and fastened to the loops of the body wire by being twisted firmly through it. The last wire is bent at right angles at each end, the bent parts going into the broken wing-bones, and thus the wings are supported. When the wings are tied, as already described, this last wire is not used. The body is now stuffed by putting in pieces of tow, about 2 in. long, and pushing each into its place with the stuffer. In this way the body is gradually formed, but the risk of over-stuffing the bird and the difficulty of giving it true form are so great, that this method is rarely used now, and only by men of experience. It is illustrated by Fig 23, where A is the body wire; B, wing-bearers; C, leg and body wires joined. Sometimes a cork is used on the body wire (as shown in Fig 24) instead of the loop, and the other wires are bolted into this. In fact, the variations in form of the wirework are many, but they all have this in common—that they are fastened as firmly together as possible, so that any one wire should be able to support the whole without allowing any shake. It is possible to carve the body out of peat and insert this into the skin, but this method is not desirable, because the bird is sure to look wooden when done, and there is no possibility of alteration. Besides, peat is a dirty thing to work with, and there is a risk of introducing some injurious insect or larva into the skin, which may sooner or later destroy it. Because of this risk it is not advisable to use peat either in stuffing or in the fitting up of the case.

Now the stuffing of the bird is complete; but before it can be put in a case it must be placed somewhere out of the way of dust and insects in order to dry, which may take a fortnight or more. If put in a case before it is thoroughly dry it will slowly rot. Before the bird is put away, notice should be taken of the colour of the feet, cere (base of mandibles), or round the eyes, for, though in the bird, now being mounted, touching up is not needed, it must be remembered that the bright colours of some birds disappear, and then the colours as the birds

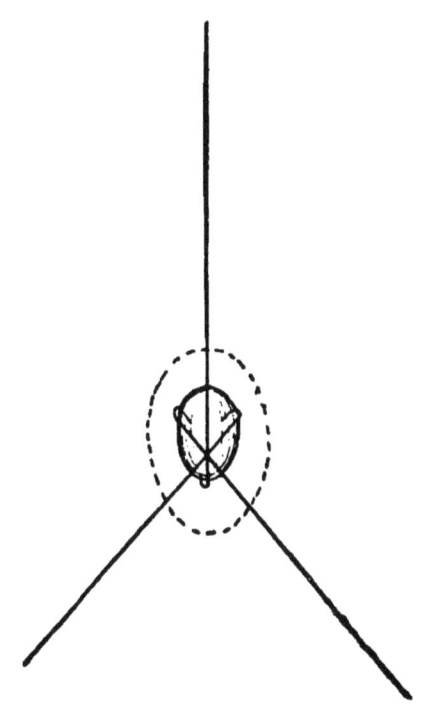

Fig. 24.—Cork Foundation for Body of Bird.

dry have to be restored with oil paint. Perhaps it is better to paint these parts before the colours fade, as they serve as good guides which prevent mistake. Best tube colours are used for the purpose, but in minute quantities, and they should be thinned with turpentine only, and applied with a small brush thinly and evenly so as not to hide the scales or scutellæ on the legs; the colours should not be glossy, for a glance at a live duck or other bird will show that the legs are not polished. Five minutes' study of a live bird will give more instruction than can possibly be given here; strive to avoid conventionality in colouring and mounting birds, and aim at imitating nature. Do not, on any account, copy stuffed specimens, for such a course is merely to perpetuate mistakes already committed.

Following are a few points to be observed in the work of stuffing birds.

As regards eyes, most little birds, up to starlings or thrushes, are very well suited with black eyes, but above that size the real iris should be matched in colour. In buying eyes, it is far better to procure uncoloured ones, known as flints, as it is a simple matter to colour them as required. The most useful sizes are: No. 3, finches; No. 5, blackbirds; Nos. 8 and 9, ducks; No. 9, crows, partridges, and jays; No. 11, gulls (small) and pheasants; Nos. 12 and 13, owls, geese, and gulls; Nos. 13 and 14, herons and hawks; Nos. 15 and 16, eagles and owls. Fig. 25 shows a few of the eyes that are usually employed for birds and mammals.

The wire used in the bodies of the birds is galvanised iron generally, and it will be found safer to err on the side of stoutness, for nothing is more annoying than to find the bird all shaking and trembling when set up. The body wire is always thinner than the leg wires. The following may be a rough guide for a commencement: No. 23, small finches; No. 21, large finches; No. 19, starlings; Nos. 16 and 17, pigeons; No. 13, crows; No. 12, owls, ducks, and hawks; No. 10, herons; Nos. 7 and 8, eagles and geese.

The positions and attitudes of birds can be learnt only from nature. It is in most cases worse than useless to go to taxidermists and copy their work. Good photographs and pictures by competent artists should be relied on in preference to the work of a taxidermist, if it is impossible to see the birds in the

STUFFING AND MOUNTING BIRDS.   37

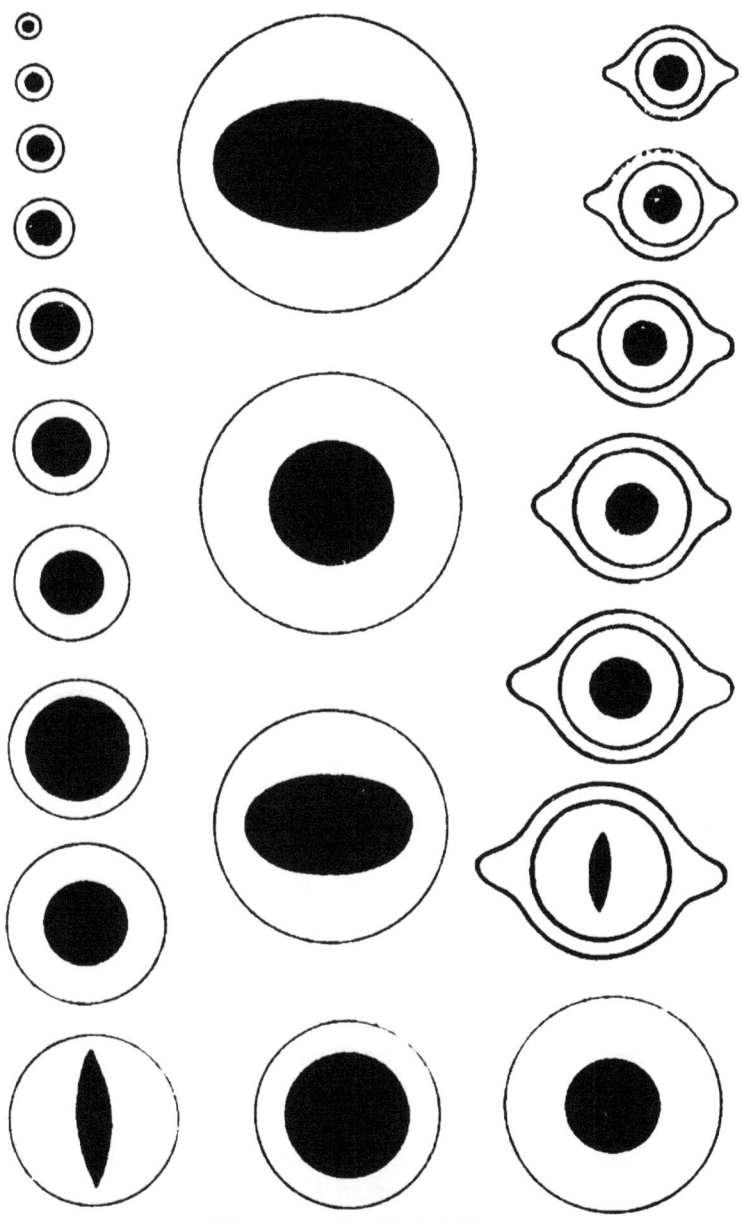

Fig. 25.—Artificial Eyes.

midst of their natural surroundings. Taxidermists, other than trained and observant naturalists, should procure some good standard work on natural history, and study the illustrations. A caged song-bird, if carefully studied, will give all necessary information with respect to small birds, and in the course of half an hour will present dozens of new attitudes which have never yet appeared in a case of stuffed birds. Notice that the legs are not as straight as drumsticks, but the heels are closer together than the feet. Five minutes spent in watching a few ducks will teach more than weeks spent in gazing into glazed cases. Ducks walk pen-toed, that is, with the toes turned inward. Their beaks are not so highly polished as those of some specimens in show-cases.

A day in the country when snow is on the ground will give an intelligent person who cares to take measurements and make drawings of footprints more object lessons in setting up birds correctly than years of haphazard work. Footprints on the mud are nature's guide for the distance and position of the feet of wading birds.

The following notes are on special subjects that reasonably may not be supposed to come under the ordinary notice of individuals.

Hawks seizing their prey have their wings raised; tail spread downwards (fanlike); body inclined to the prey; head and neck also bent towards the prey; eyes glaring, and feathers round head raised; and claws extended.

Birds when flying have their wings extended; tail spread in a line with the body; claws shut; and feet close to the breast.

Woodpeckers are best shown climbing a tree, with the tail resting upon the bark.

Nightjars generally sit lengthways upon a branch, and not, as most birds, at right angles to it.

Gulls look most unnatural if their legs are bent

like those of most other birds. Only a very small portion of the feathered part should be seen, and their legs should be quite straight.

When a bird is surprised or alarmed, the wing on the side from which the alarm has come will be slightly raised, as will that side of the drooping tail, and the head will be turned in that direction.

The webs of ducks, gulls, etc., can be kept from shrivelling by fitting a piece of stiff card, cut to the exact shape, between each two toes, and then fastening it to the board by tin tacks or gimp pins.

Birds in flight, as mentioned on p. 38, have their wings extended. To extend the wings, insert a pointed wire below the wrist joint (K, Fig. 16, p. 19), and let it pass along the underside of this bone (really there are two bones together). Be careful about the next joint. Now let it pass along the two bones that were met when skinning the wing; lift up the wing at the angle desired, and force the wire into the body. This will be found sufficient to support the wing. Several other wires may pass under the larger feathers into the body if thought necessary, but these are only temporary, and will afterwards be removed. The wire to support the bird will be entered under the wing on one side, pushed right through the bird and firmly bolted into the body under the other wing. There are plenty of feathers here to hide it. Sometimes this supporting wire is put under the tail.

Frequently birds require cleaning in some part. Benzoline should be used for this purpose. It should be applied by means of cotton-wool, frequently changed, in the same direction as the feathers lie. When all appears clean, plenty of plaster-of-paris should be applied, and when this is caked together, it should be shaken off and more applied. When all is dry, a few taps should make the feathers spring up; if not, arrange them with the feather pliers. Blood is best removed with water, followed by benzoline and plaster. The most obstinate cases will yield to water; then apply turpentine, next benzoline, and then plaster. If all is not satisfactory when quite dry, repeat the cleaning.

To restore the head of a bird to its original white colour, perhaps years after it was mounted, first well dust it with feathers and then adopt the method just explained. Or try the following American plan: Dissolve a piece of pipeclay the size of a walnut in rather less than 1 pt. of warm water; well wash the bird with a soft flannel dipped in the liquid and well soaped with Sunlight soap. When clean, wash again in clean water, and roll in a cloth to dry. Then hold in front of a fire and beat briskly with a folded towel. Do not adopt this method with a valuable skin, but after the washing apply benzoline, then plaster, and beat with feathers in preference to a towel. Otherwise, the bird will probably dry rough.

Covering the birds with pure benzoline will kill all insects, and directly it has evaporated the specimens should be put in a case, where they will last indefinitely. The benzolines of the oilshops generally contain paraffin, and this will do more harm than good. The specimen is then enclosed till dry in a frame covered with muslin, something like a meat safe. This allows the air to enter freely, but keeps away the moths. When dry the specimen should be cased. A solution in alcohol or methylated spirit of corrosive sublimate (bichloride of mercury) is good both for birds and mammals, and poured over the feathers or fur prevents further attacks of insects. The spirit soon evaporates, leaving the poison behind, and no insect will touch a specimen thus treated. To make the solution of corrosive sublimate, agitate this in the solvent to form a saturated solution, and then reduce it by adding more alcohol until a black feather dipped in and allowed to dry shows no white deposit upon its filaments. This, poured over the specimen, will defy the attacks of both insects and mildew. But it is too dangerous to be used on uncased specimens. Turpentine may be used for animals, and if these are to be uncased, a good brushing to remove the dust, followed by a thorough covering with turpentine, once, or at most twice, a year, will keep them right for many years.

The method of making the corrosive sublimate solution recommended by Dr. Oliver Davie (an American) is as follows:—To make 2 qt. of the solution place 1½ oz. of corrosive sublimate in 1 qt. of alcohol. Allow the mixture to stand for a short time, and then (as the alcohol does not take up all the sublimate) pour off the liquid from that which settles at the bottom. Now add 1 qt. of water to that which has been poured off, and the solution is ready for use. The solution may be poured over sufficient clean white sand in which the bird skin is buried for from twelve to twenty-four hours. For skins of animals the solution may be made somewhat stronger, and applied by pouring it through an earthenware teapot. Smaller or larger quantities can, of course, be made by decreasing or increasing the ingredients. A black feather, as noted on p. 40, may be used for testing the strength of the solution.

Stuffed birds are not, as a general rule, dyed. The less the feathers are disturbed, and the less artificial cleaning that is done, the greater will be the gloss. The natural gloss of the feathers depends upon the arrangement of the barbules and plumules of the feather. During cleaning, it is impossible to avoid unfastening the small hooklets on these plumules, and thus destroying the natural gloss of the feather.

Instructions on mounting stuffed birds in cases, and also on constructing the cases, are given in Chapter VIII., pp. 149 to 156.

Specimens of apparently animated nature, preserved and arranged mainly as ornaments by the art of the taxidermist, take so many and such varied forms that it would be almost impossible to enumerate them, much less to describe them; of course, the usual plan is to enclose stuffed birds in glass cases, but they lend themselves to more than one form of ornament. One of their most tasteful applications is in the decoration of screens. All such screens are more or less useful as well as being ornamental; the one most commonly seen is the hand screen, and this will be described first. The

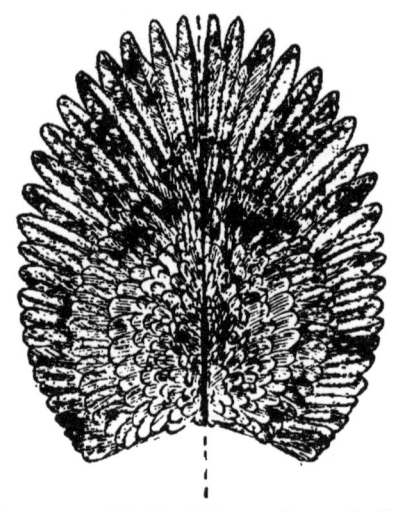

Fig. 26.—Bird's Wings Spread Out.

birds most suitable for these are gulls, hooded crows, carrion crows, owls, and hawks.

Procure one of these birds—with unbroken wings if possible—and proceed to skin it by an opening on the back, according to the instructions given in Chapter I. Having cleaned the bones satisfactorily, cut off the wings and tail, and fasten them temporarily to a piece of wood or the back of a door by means of pointed wires, pins, etc. Arrange them so that they form a symmetrical pattern. Sometimes their inner parts are made to meet all the way down, as in Fig. 26. Fine needles or entomological pins (see p. 136) passing through the webs may be used to spread the quill feathers into the form of an oval, and card braces or binding cotton may supplement these to ensure all the feathers lying down in their places.

Wiring is not absolutely necessary, though it is a good plan to use a wire for each wing, entering it as near the tip as possible, and letting it pass inside the skin down through the butt. This, besides giving more rigidity, is of assistance in fastening the wing to its final block. The tail is also spread in a

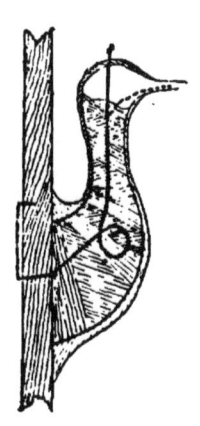

Fig. 27.—Section of Bird's Head on Screen.

similar manner. The head and breast are now stuffed either by loose stuffing, or, preferably, by binding tow round a piece of wire, in which has been formed a ring, to prevent the wire drawing through. This is made sufficiently clear by the section (Fig. 27). The wrapped end, of course, enters the skin, and the naked end of the wire which projects from the tow is forced through the skull, which necessitates its being pointed; or it may lie in the mouth, as shown by the dotted line in Fig. 27, when it need not be pointed. By means of the other end of the wire the bird is fastened to a flat piece of wood. Bore a hole in this wood, pass the wire through, and pull it until the skin rests upon the board. Then bend the wire and bolt it into the back of the wood to hold the whole securely. Now pass a knitting needle or pricker under the feathers resting upon the wood whilst arranging them in order. Bend the head sideways, if preferred, and, should any feathers rise, which is rather improbable, bind cotton around them. The wire projecting from the top of the head should next be cut off, and the beak closed, after which the work should be placed away, out of the dust, to dry. The eyes should be inserted before the stuffing is done; for instructions on this and other points, see the earlier part of this chapter. Some taxidermists, instead of leaving the breast open, and merely resting upon the board, stitch it up after stuffing it, but the final results are not so satisfactory, as the outside feathers do not spread out so well to hide the junction of the breast and wings.

While the wings, etc., are drying, procure the screen handle, which should be turned from a piece of wood about 10 in. long and $\frac{5}{8}$ in. square, and should have its top left square and unturned for from 1 in. to $1\frac{1}{2}$ in. This square piece has a slit cut in it for its full length to take a flat piece of wood to which the wings, tail, and head are fastened finally, and has two holes drilled through it, as shown by Fig. 28, by means of which to secure the flat piece or block. The block, about $\frac{1}{4}$ in. thick, will vary in length and breadth with the size of the bird, and may be left rectangular, or, preferably, be cut to an oval. Fit the handle and block together by glue and pegs, driven through the two holes drilled for this purpose. Then finish the handle by staining and polishing, or enamelling, or gilding, and, when quite dry and hard, cover it with paper to keep it clean. Information on the points just mentioned, namely, the finishing of the woodwork, is hardly within the scope of this book; but these subjects are treated fully in a companion WORK handbook.

When the wings, etc., are quite set and dry, they are placed upon the block attached to the handle and secured to it by glue, wires, tacks, etc. The wings are fastened first, and attention must be paid to their position with regard to the handle—that is

Fig. 28.—Handle for Bird Screen.

to say, if one forms an angle with the handle the other must form a similar angle.

Glue the tail, place it upon the wings, and secure with wires, pins, or tacks, the feathers thus radiating

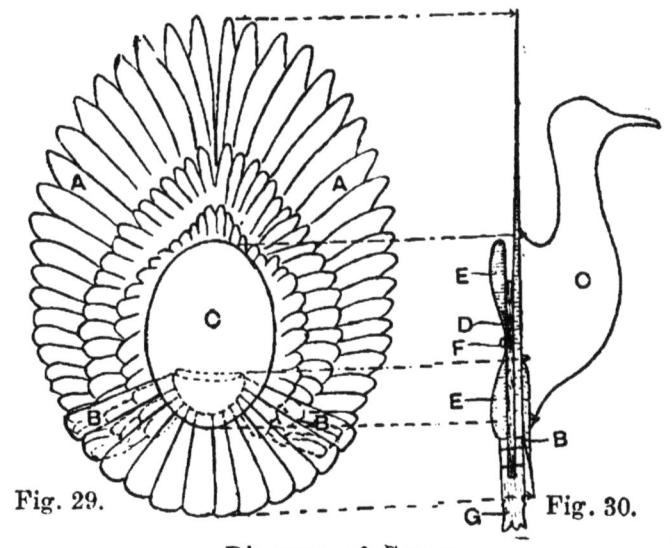

Fig. 29. Fig. 30.

Diagram of Screen.

round the bottom of the wings. The breast, etc., is glued upon these, and the head wire, which is passed through the block, pulled well home and bolted securely into the back of the block. Over the back of the block glue silk, satin, or velvet, in order to hide the wires and to provide a finish; but a much better plan is to cut an oval piece of thin wood or card and upon it place two thicknesses of cotton-wool. This is then covered with silk, etc.,

Fig. 31.—Turned Base for Screen.

the edges of which are pulled over and fixed down. The block is covered with glue, the prepared back

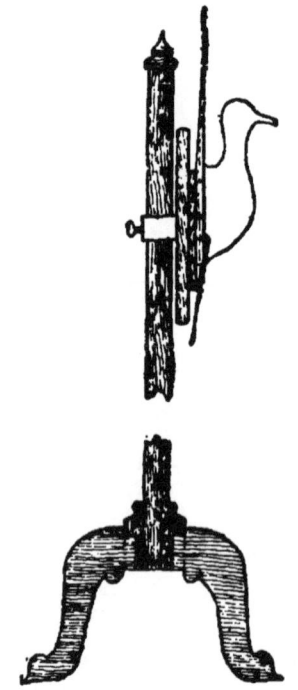

Fig. 32.—Screen with Stuffed Bird.

placed upon it, and an ornamental brass pin as used in upholstery forced through the silk, wadding, and board into the block, thus pressing the wadding down in the centre and making the padding apparent. In Figs. 29 and 30, A A represent the wings, B B denote the tail, C the position of the breast, D the block, E E the padded back, F the fancy brass pin, and G the handle.

Larger birds, such as herons and large gulls, may be treated in a similar manner, but, instead of being fixed to a handle, may be provided at the back with two wires, by means of which they are hung to the bars of an unused fire-grate in summer, thus forming a much more effective grate screen than the common pictorial card or paper screens.

For a useful as well as an ornamental fire-screen, the back may be of polished wood, upon which is fixed a fancy brass ring, to enable it to be moved up or down a turned and polished upright rod rising from a turned base (Fig. 31), or from carved legs (Fig. 32). The latter figure shows the fire-screen complete.

Other screens are sometimes seen resembling cases with glass fronts and backs, and filled with brightly-coloured foreign birds. These may be made to slide along a rod at each side, and may be fixed at any height by thumbscrews, or they may have fixed feet provided with casters. Bamboo does admirably for these cases, the bright markings of the bamboo harmonising well with the brilliant colours of the birds. A handle is usually fixed at the top of the screens, by which they can be moved as required.

CHAPTER III.

SKINNING AND STUFFING MAMMALS.

HAVING followed the directions given in the previous chapters on skinning, stuffing, and mounting birds, slightly more difficult work may be attempted, namely, the setting up of mammals. The tools for this purpose are the same as those mentioned on pp. 9-15 for the treatment of birds. In fact, with the addition of a larger stuffing-iron (see Figs. 11 and 12, p. 14), made from a broken fencing foil, or from boxwood, about 18 in. or 2 ft. long, the tools used in skinning and mounting a humming-bird answer equally well with a wolf or a larger mammal.

The preservatives recommended for birds (pp. 16 and 17) will also be found quite as applicable to mammals as large as a cat; but beyond this, something of a rather different character may well be used. The best composition is simply a mixture of 4 parts of powdered burnt alum with 1 part of powdered saltpetre. The experience of years guarantees this to give complete satisfaction, being thoroughly effective in its action and harmless to the user.

Many taxidermists still use nothing but powdered alum (known as "hards"), but alum readily absorbs moisture and becomes liquid; therefore, if the specimen on which it has been used is placed in a damp situation, it naturally follows that the alum, owing to its affinity for water, will soon render the specimen damp, and thus quickly destroy its beauty.

Ordinary table salt is used, either alone or mixed with alum, by some foreign taxidermists, especially Americans. Carbolic acid may be used with good results, but for all-round excellence nothing can equal the mixture of burnt alum and saltpetre.

Probably the first attempt will be made upon some small and easily obtained mammal, and for this reason the squirrel will be taken as an example. Having the tools well within reach, the first thing is to take measurements. It is easy to stretch a fresh skin, during the process of stuffing, out of all proportion and resemblance, and therefore the

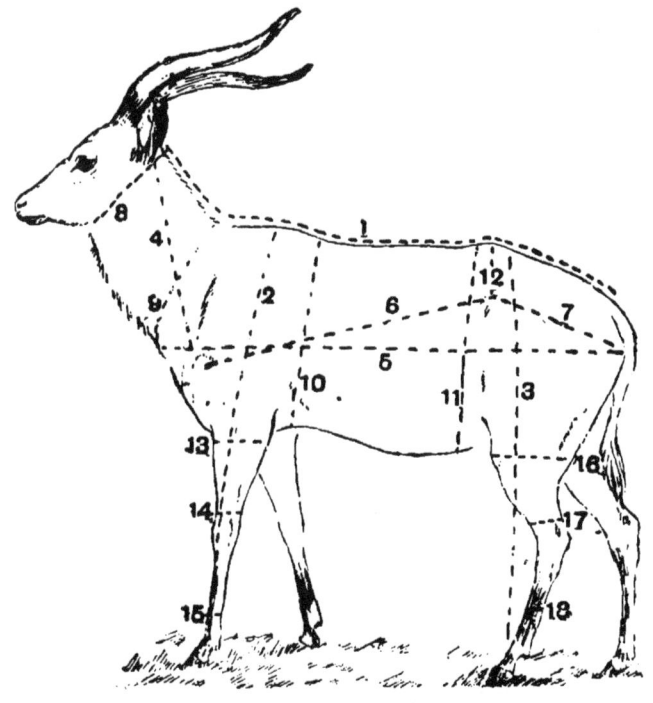

Fig. 33.—Measurement of Waterbuck.

measurements must on no account be omitted. It is not necessary to make the full series of measurements on a squirrel, so, for future reference, the measurement of a waterbuck (Fig. 33) will be considered. The measurements are:—1. Head to tail, made by a tape measure close to the skin. 2. Height at shoulders, most easily made by a straight rule. 3. Height at back legs, made by a straight rule.

D

4. Length of neck, from ear to collar, made by tape measure. 5. Length of body, from chest to rump. 6. Femur to humerus. 7. Femur to rump. 8. Circumference of neck, near the head. 9. Circumference of neck, near the chest. 10. Circumference of body near the fore legs. 11. Circumference of body, near the hind legs. 12. Humerus to humerus, over the back. 13, 14, 15. Circumference of fore legs. 16, 17, 18. Circumference of hind legs. The distance from ear to ear must also be taken.

The circumference of the head should be taken in several places, also the distance between the fore legs and between the hind legs. Any particular curves desired may easily be obtained by bending thin strips of lead along the mammal before skinning, and applying these to the outside of the specimen as the stuffing is progressing.

It will be found a good plan to make a rough sketch of the animal, and insert these measurements, placing below any remarks, notes, etc. Then, if necessary, the skin may be put away and stuffed accurately years afterwards. Of use, also, in mounting the specimen is a photograph of the animal before skinning, and, if possible, whilst it was alive; this, of course, is not always convenient.

In the case of the squirrel, it may be sufficient to measure:—1. From the nose to the tail. 2. Length of the tail. 3. Circumference of the body.

The skinning now may be commenced. A piece of paper is spread upon the table, and upon this the squirrel is placed, belly upwards, with its head towards the skinner. Enter the point of the knife between the fore legs, and cut in a straight line to near the vent. The dotted line in Fig. 34 shows the cut. Be careful when past the ribs that the knife does not cut through the thin walls of the abdomen, or the bowels will protrude and cause trouble. Proceed to separate the skin on each side, and be careful about pulling for fear of stretching the skin, keeping the edge of the knife inclined more to the flesh than to the skin. Freely use the plaster-of-paris as advised on p. 18 when skinning birds. There are two

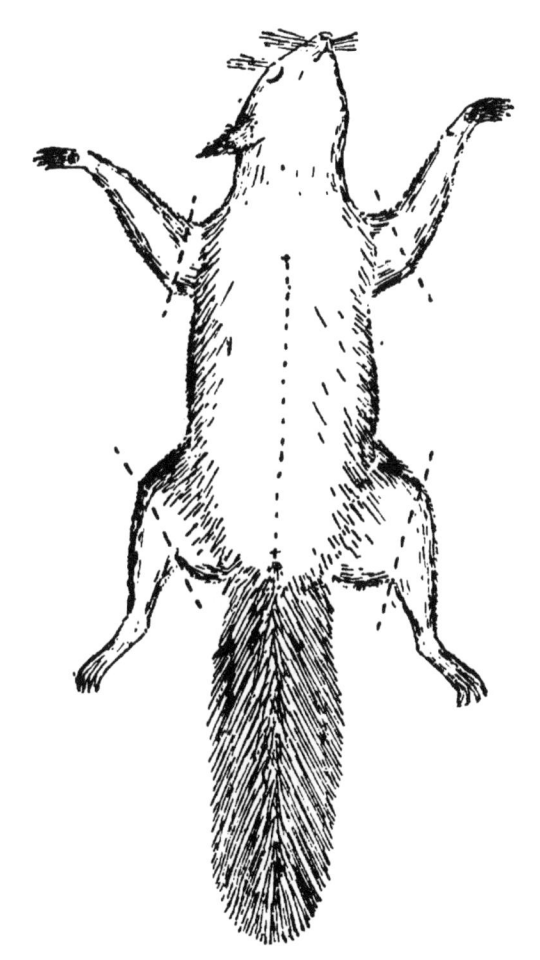

Fig. 34.—Squirrel.

modes of procedure, one being to release the hind legs and tail, to hang the body upon the hook (Figs. 14 and 15, p. 15), and go in a straight course to the head, and there sever, returning thence to the tail; the other is by releasing the fore legs and cutting through the neck, to suspend the body from the shoulder, etc., and then skin downwards, returning to the neck and skinning to the head, and then severing. There is little to choose between the methods. Remember, there must be no pulling, as when skinning a rabbit for culinary purposes, but the knife must be used constantly, cutting and scraping all the time. The legs must be cut at the joints (see Fig. 34) either by using the point of the knife, or, far more easily, by the side cutters (Figs. 5 and 6, p. 12).

The tail in most small mammals can be skinned without cutting the skin by holding one end firmly and pushing (not pulling) the skin completely off. In the case of the squirrel, if the thickest part of the tail be held firmly with the flat pliers (Fig. 7, p. 12), and the following part be placed in the bellhangers' pliers (Fig. 8, p. 12), which are closed with just sufficient firmness to prevent the skin doubling in, it will be found that when the two tools are separated with some force the tail will slide quite out to the tip without turning the skin. The bell-hangers' pliers are a great convenience here, but not a necessity, as the fingers and thumb of the right hand will answer instead, while the butt of the tail is held by the other hand or by the flat-nosed pliers. In the case of the fox, the butt of the tail is best held by being placed in a vice, and then, by encircling the next part by the hollows of a pair of carpenters' nail pincers, a sharp pull or a series of jerks with these pincers will cause it to slide. Or the tail may be held between the door and its jamb instead of the vice, and be made to slide by holding the next part between the thumb and two fingers of both hands, and then pulling or jerking. It is only necessary to see that the skin does not turn inside out. Still, it is trying to some fingers, as at times the tail holds firmly and some strength is required.

It is necessary to free the limbs and head from

flesh. Starting, then, to skin the skull, very little progress will be made before two gristly or cartilaginous bodies will be met with, one on each side. These are the ears, and should be freed by cutting *into* the flesh towards the bone. By carefully cutting all round, about ½ in. more progress is made when two more stoppages are met with, one on each side again. These are the eyes, and the greatest care must be taken now. The cuts must be very minute and the hand very light. Very soon the skin appears almost transparent, and the dark eye is seen beneath. This skin should be carefully cut through, keeping close to the eye. Now the most difficult part is reached. The lips, upper and lower, must be skinned quite to their very edges. This is a tedious affair, for the cuts must be by hair-breadths only at a time. This is called "pocketing" the lips. It may simplify matters to cut through the cartilage of the nose down to the bone, as then more freedom is gained in pocketing the lips and skinning the nose. Much care must be taken, for the skin of the nose is extremely thin, and is the worst place possible for a slip to be made. If the hand holding the skin has the forefinger inside and against the lips, the cuts can be much better directed. Doubtless, before reaching quite so far, several small oval-shaped bodies will be met with on the sides of the upper lip. These are the roots of the whiskers, and, if the cuts are carelessly made, and these roots cut through, the whiskers will fall out and cannot easily be replaced. However, assuming that the lip has been skinned quite to the edge, and the cartilage of the nose separated from the skin, the next thing is to pocket the lower lip. This is more difficult in a squirrel because the place is so confined; but by proceeding slowly, by minute cuts, and feeling and directing with the finger inside the skin, it is quite possible to get quite to the edge. The result of not separating the cartilage of the nose from the skin, or only partially doing so, will be shown by an unsightly shrivelling when the squirrel dries, instead of the plumpness and fulness seen in a live squirrel's nose.

The head is now quite skinned and requires cleaning, but measurements must again be made before the flesh is removed. Measure the circumference in several places, notice where the swelling of the cheeks begins, the gradual slope towards the eyes, and the shape of the cheeks—not bulging out like half apples. Having made a rough sketch and put in the measurements and anything else noticed, the flesh should now be all removed. The tongue and neighbouring flesh is quickly removed in one piece by a cut along each side of the lower jaw, and quite close to the bone. If this were a fox's tongue, or the tongue of an animal to be represented with open mouth, it might be required for subsequent operations, such as casting from it, or modelling from it, etc., and would therefore have to be saved for a time, probably in salt and water, or by covering it with plenty of the preservative. On the top of many skulls is a ridge of bone, on each side of which is a thick pad of flesh. By starting at this ridge and keeping close to the bone it is possible to remove most of this in one piece. The eyes are readily removed with the awl or with the brain-spoon (Fig. 9, p. 13). Beneath the eye is a bony ridge, and below this the fleshy pad forming the cheek. By cutting with the point of the knife along this ridge quite to the lower jaw and then commencing at the lower edge of the jawbone, most of the cheek comes away in one piece. Now the top of the palate must be removed, for between this and the skull lie the brains. In the squirrel the knife or scissors will do this, but in a larger animal a small saw or a hatchet, or at least a chisel and a mallet, will be called into play. The brains are now easily removed, very probably almost unbroken. There still remain some small pieces of flesh, which these cuts have missed, and every bit that is possible must come away. The cleaner the skull is the better the finish will be. Now the fore legs must be freed from flesh. No difficulty will be met with in skinning quite down past the wrist until the toes are seen. Nothing will be gained by going any farther, but in the case of a dog or fox further work would be required as described subsequently. There is but little flesh about the wrist, so nothing need be done here, but about the two upper bones (ulna and radius, corresponding to the part of the human arms between the wrist and elbow) some masses of flesh will be seen, and these can all be removed by two or three cuts. Repeat with all the legs, and now give all, both skin and bone, a dressing with the preservative. Do not neglect the inside of the skull nor the tail, using the knitting needle, a piece of wire, or some similar thing to get the preservative well down.

The squirrel is now ready for stuffing. Before, however, describing this process there are several things necessary to be noticed, which may now be mentioned.

Most of the carnivora (flesh-eating animals) give out a rather strong effluvium when their bodies are disturbed, and for this reason it is always the better plan to plug up the orifices (throat, nostrils, vent, etc.) of the animal with cotton-wool before skinning. This is especially the case with the weasel family (weasels, stoats, polecats, ferrets, etc.), because near the root of the tails of the members of this family are yellowish glands for the secretion of a most pungent fluid, the disgusting odour of which will cling to the room for a long while if this simple precaution be neglected and the knife should happen to pierce them.

Insectivora (insect- and fruit-eating animals) and graminivora (grass-eating animals) decompose more quickly than carnivora, and this is shown by the skin along the abdomen turning green and the hair or fur "slipping" or coming away in large quantities.

When skinning, keep as much as possible of the flesh and fat upon the body, and as little as possible upon the skin, or in subsequently removing these the skin may be stretched; but guard against cutting the skin.

Males and pouched animals should be opened on the side of the organ if it is necessary to retain these characteristics.

As regards the feet of dogs and foxes, it will be found almost impossible to skin the leg and foot to the toes from the inside. Therefore, upon reaching the wrist from the inside a stop must be made, and the bone cleaned and preserved. Then the skin is returned to its original position, and a cut made from the outside, beginning at the back of the wrist and going across the pad, the inside of which will be found to be a mass of firm fat. This must all be cut away, and with a little care the knife can easily be made to pass almost to the tips of the toes and upwards to the wrist. Although little flesh may be removed, this separation must not be omitted nor done carelessly, or the part neglected will eventually shrivel. The skin and bones are then well dressed with preservative, and the removed fat, etc., are replaced with chopped tow, or with clay or putty. When neatly sewn up with strong thread, close inspection should not be able to ascertain that it has been opened.

Monkeys are difficult subjects, for the hands and feet must be opened on the undersides, as shown by dotted lines in Fig. 35. They are then skinned quite to the tips of their fingers and toes through these cuts, and all the flesh noticed must be carefully removed. Their bodies are best opened along the back, because most of the hair lies there, and

Skinning and Stuffing Mammals. 57

also because their front is generally made the show-piece of the specimen.

Having turned the skin to its normal position, by returning the legs and head into their skins, the flesh which has been taken away must be replaced by tow. Here again many methods are in vogue. The usual plan is to place putty or clay into the pockets of the lips, and then with the stuffing-iron to force pieces of tow up into the skull, by the sides

Fig. 35.—Hand of Monkey.

of the face and into the mouth, modelling this into shape as well as possible. This method, however common it may be, must be strongly condemned, for it is impossible to make a really artistic piece of work thus. If the modelling appears perfect at one time, during the subsequent drying a certain amount of shrinkage must take place, and this, to an observant naturalist, is at once apparent by the unequal appearance of the two sides of the face. The method which can be recommended on all grounds is to replace the flesh of the head with an unyielding substance such as plaster-of-paris, stuffing the rest of the body with tow. In the larger animals it is the practice of the best workmen to form a framework of wood and iron, and on this skeleton to make a body of tow, wood-wool, etc., then over this body to place a layer of clay, plaster, pulped paper, or a mixture of the three, and in this to carefully model the various superficial muscles. When this model, or manikin, is complete, the skin is stretched over and finished by sewing, nailing, etc.

It may be advantageous to return to the squirrel rather more in detail. An excellent method of treating the head, large or small, is the following: In the orbits and the places where large masses of flesh have been taken away, pieces of tow for small mammals, or of peat (treated with corrosive sublimate to kill insects) carved roughly into shape, for larger ones, are fixed, being kept in place by thread, string, or wire. Some tow, in long pieces, is forced into the hollow of the skull, and made equal in diameter to the neck. Some more is now wrapped round this, special attention being paid to the junction of the head and neck. This artificial neck serves to hold the head, in the case of the squirrel, during the next process. Some plaster-of-paris is now prepared by sprinkling the plaster into water and stirring into a cream-like mass. With this the whole head is covered and quickly smoothed into shape with an ordinary table knife or putty knife. A sketch of the head was made previously to the flesh being removed, and upon this various measurements, notes, etc., were recorded. These are applied to the head now in hand, more plaster being put on or smoothed away until the whole is an exact reproduction of the head as it came from the skin. In a very few minutes the plaster sets, but even then any alteration may be made, if necessary, by scraping with a knife, or, in larger cases, by using a rasp. Some putty is put into the "pockets" of the lips and round the nose, and then the whole is forced into the skin. Two small wires may be pushed up the nostrils and into the skull, to keep the nose in position, leaving, of course, enough to withdraw them by when the squirrel is dry. The putty may be pushed to the edge of the skin, if out of place, by putting the knitting needle or stuffing-iron through the eyelids, and it may again be modelled into shape by the fingers from the outside. The great advantage of this method is that, the plaster being unyielding, shrinkage cannot possibly take place. And complex though the process appears in print, it will probably be found, in practice, to take but five or ten minutes at the outside—very little longer, in fact, than when using tow alone—while satisfaction is assured. The eyes may now be inserted and fixed upon a bed of putty, or may be left until later. Guard against leaving the eyes too staring. It is advisable here to refer to the information given on these points with reference to birds (see Chapter II.).

If it is found very difficult to close the mouth of the specimen, one, or perhaps two, faults have been committed. Either the lips have not been pocketed to their edges, or the putty has not been pressed to the extreme edge of the lips. The lips must be skinned quite to their edges, as advised above. Then the putty can be worked to these edges, and when the skin, etc., dries and contracts, this putty will keep the external and internal skins apart. An extra means of keeping the lips together is to pin them through. In the case of larger animals the lips are sometimes sewn together, and the stitches removed when the specimens are dry.

Before the skull is returned to the skin, and while the plaster is setting, the six wires can be got ready —four for the limbs, one for the body, and a thin one for the tail. A list of suitable wires scarcely can be given, because they will vary very much indeed with the age and position of the mammal.

However, an examination of a number of finished mammals discloses the following:—

>No. 18 Gauge suitable for weasels.
>,, 17 ,, ,, ,, squirrels and stoats.
>,, 15 ,, ,, ,, ferrets and polecats.
>,, 12 & 13 ,, ,, ,, cats and small dogs.
>,, 9 & 10 ,, ,, ,, foxes and larger dogs.
>,, 7 & 8 ,, ,, ,, still larger dogs and wolves.

It is much better to err on the side of stoutness, if at all; for nothing is worse than to find the specimen

Fig. 36.—Bones of Animal's Hind Leg.

wobbling and trembling when finished and set up. The body wire will be about 12 in. long, the tail wire, thinner, about the same length, and the leg wires 8 in. or 9 in. long. Point one end of the body and leg wires and both ends of the tail wire with a file, giving them triangular or bayonet-shaped points. Now take the body wire and, at about an inch from the blunt end, commence to wrap pieces of tow firmly round it to form an artificial body. Continue this wrapping till the false body is about as long and rather less in diameter than the real body was—remember the neck is already formed. Turn up the blunt end of the wire as advised when making the body for the bird (Fig. 17, p. 26). Push the pointed ends of the leg wires into the soles or pads of the feet, and let them travel along the back of the bones; wrap some tow round bones and wires, binding both together to represent the flesh. The hind leg has the most character in it, and requires careful work. In it the wrapping on the front side of the bone (tibia) is very thin. Remember that this part corresponds to the part of the human leg from the knee to the ankle, and that the human " shin " lies close to the skin. The muscles lie mainly at the back, and consequently most of the tow must be there. The thigh is flat inside and rounded outside.

In a larger mammal it will be particularly neces-

Fig. 37.—Artificial Hind Leg

sary to notice the tendon of Achilles—the thick strong cord which, at its lower extremity, is joined to the calcaneum—in other words, the " ham string," which rises upwards from " the point of the hock." This tendon is most easily represented in a large subject by drilling a hole through the calcaneum and through this passing a piece of copper wire. This wire is then wrapped with tow to the diameter of the original cord, and the free end is fastened to the tibia. When the skin is returned to its normal position, a stitch or two through the hollow space left between the tendon and the bone will draw both sides of the skin together and give a realistic appearance to this part which mere stuffing cannot give (see Figs. 36 and 37).

The false body now is placed in the skin, the pointed end of the wire being forced through the centre of the skull. Pass the sharp ends of the leg wires through the artificial body and secure them exactly as the leg wires of the bird were secured. Now take the tail wire and force it through the rear end of the body, letting it come out at the back against the tail, which may have had a little tow put in previously. It is an easy matter to pass it up to the end of the tail and then quite through the skin. The internal end, which was purposely pointed, is to be bent downwards into the body, and will thus hold firmly (see Fig 38). The body has been made rather thinner than the natural body to enable tow, cut up in small pieces, to be pushed, by means of the stuffing-iron, between the body and the skin. Begin at the chest and make the shoulders and chest right. Examine the work frequently to see if the proper shape and curves are obtained. Having bent the legs, etc., into the required position, and being satisfied that all is correct here, this part may be left and the hind quarters attended to. Then the body is modelled in the same manner, the circumference compared with the preliminary measurements, and finally sewn up by the stitch already described and illustrated (Fig 18, p. 28).

For stitching anything larger than the squirrel probably the triangular-pointed glover's needle will be preferred; this may be forced through a thick skin by a "sailmaker's palm," or something similar.

Now obtain a piece of wood or branch and fix the squirrel in the chosen position by bolting the wires as illustrated in Fig 19, p. 29. Notice that the heels of most mammals go closer together than their toes. If possible, obtain two squirrels, retaining one as a copy from which to model the other. Especially about the mouth, lips, and nose will this be useful, for more will be learnt in finishing one in this way than in trying a dozen times without a copy to get the correct expression. These directions will serve perfectly for any mammal up to the size of a collie dog or wolf.

Figs 39 and 40 illustrate two other methods of wiring mammals which are used by those who prefer

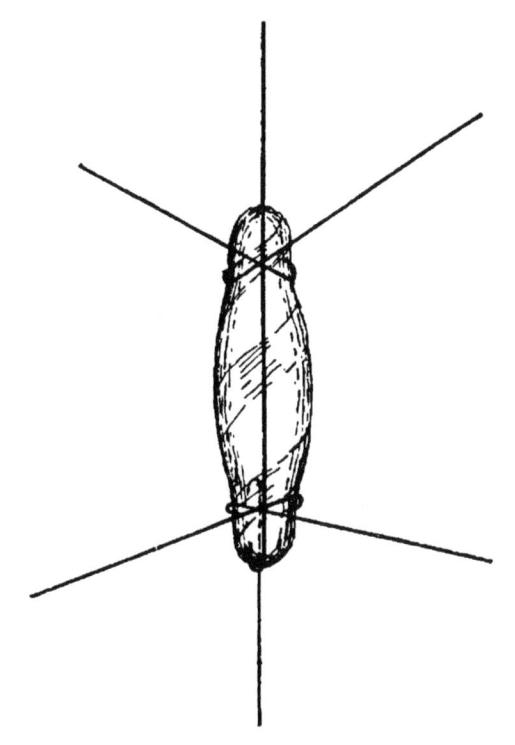

Fig. 38.—Body for Mammal.

loose stuffing. In Fig 39 the wires are formed on a similar plan to those given for loose-stuffing a bird (see pp. 32 to 34). The body and tail wires are in one, and towards the end of the part intended for the head a loop is formed. This loop will lie, when in the skin, at the shoulders, and through it the wires from the fore legs will pass and be firmly twisted round. Lower down another loop will be formed to lie in the neighbourhood of the hips. Through this the wires from the hind legs will pass and be fastened by twisting. In Fig. 40 another variation is shown. Two ordinary bottle corks are obtained and cut to correspond in length with the width of the shoulders and hips respectively. They are then fastened together at the same distance as the hips are from the shoulders, measuring from the carcase of the squirrel. The figure clearly shows how the ends of this wire are bolted into the corks. All four leg wires

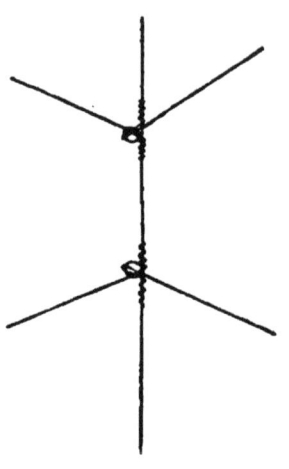

Fig. 39.—Wiring for Loose Stuffing of Mammal.

pass completely through the corks, and have the pointed ends bent back again to make them firm. Two other wires for the head and tail (both ends of these require pointing) pass through the corks, and are also made fast by bolting the ends into the corks. A reference to the figure will make this plain. This is certainly an improvement upon Fig. 39, though it entails much more work. Neither, however, can compare with the method illustrated by Fig. 38, either for ease, quickness, or accuracy.

Mammals with open mouths (snarling) have the lips raised, showing the gums and inside of the lips.

These will require to be painted (see the notes on p. 35), but the colours must not be made too deep. The teeth may be cleaned with weak muriatic acid. The teeth of foxes, dogs, etc., can be bleached by washing well in warm soda and water, rinsing, and applying a mixture of 1 oz. of hydrogen peroxide and twenty to thirty drops of strong ammonia; apply this often during a period of ten hours, and then wash. If required, polish with a wet cloth dipped in finely powdered pumice-stone, and lastly

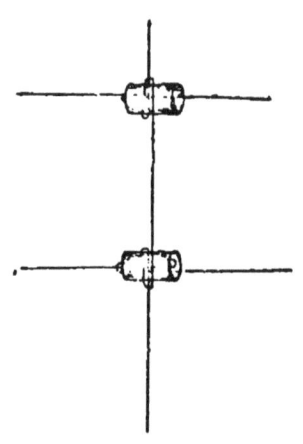

Fig. 40.—Wiring for Loose Stuffing of Mammal.

with whiting and a little warm soapsuds. Allow to dry very slowly.

Very little information can be given about the attitudes of mammals, but notice that an animal rarely shows its emotions in its face without a corresponding action of its limbs and body, and, as these actions vary with different species, it is impossible to give a general rule; but much may be learnt by watching a dog or a cat. When the cat is angry its ears are almost level with the skin of the head; its back is arched as highly as possible; its hair is slightly raised, mouth open, showing teeth. Probably one foot is half raised ready to strike, the other legs being almost straight, and its tail has a peculiar curve—upwards for about a quarter of its length, the remainder hanging vertically downwards—or the tail is perhaps more commonly seen lashing from side to side. If a cat is frightened its back and ears may be as above, but its hair will be standing on end. If it is pleased its back will be arched, but not so highly as when angry, its ears will be raised, and the tail will be upright, and at the same time it may be rubbing its head and body in a peculiar manner against the object it desires to caress. In the dog nearly every action is different. Wagging the tail is ex-

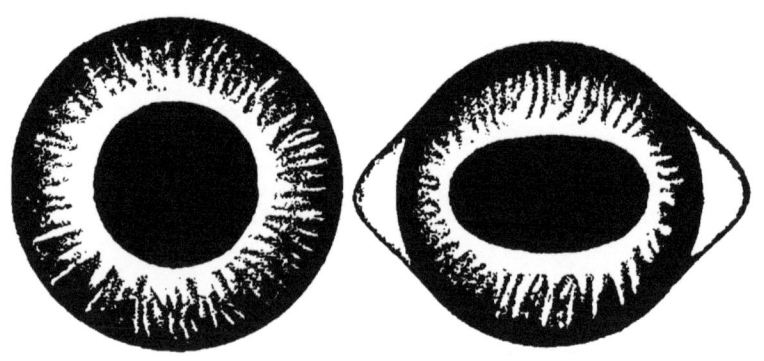

Fig. 41. Fig. 42.
Artificial Eyes.

pressive of joy, while a stiff, erect tail may mean attention; but if its hair is on end at the same time it certainly shows anger. If attacking, every muscle is drawn tight, its hair is like bristles, tail stiff and erect, limbs are straight, ears lie down, and the lips are drawn back well out of reach of its own teeth. The ears are raised at attention or when challenging. The above is given simply to show that nature, not taxidermists, must be used as a guide. In the last paragraph on p. 36 some points are emphasised that are equally applicable here.

Fig. 41 shows a veined eye, and Fig. 42 a veined and cornered eye suitable for the larger mammals.

Skinning and Stuffing Mammals. 67

Other and smaller eyes are illustrated by Fig. 25, p. 37.

From the body of a mole a pretty little purse may be made. Make a cut along the belly from the front legs to the hind ones; then separate the skin along each side as far as possible. Cut the hind legs from the body, then the tail, and skin the body up to the fore legs. Cut these free, and skin up to the tip of the nose. Separate the whole body by cutting at the base of the skull. Remove the brain, and clean all the flesh from the skull and feet. The tail is as well left alone. Then dress with Browne's preservative (p. 17), and put some putty round the nose and

Fig. 43.—Moleskin Purse.

mouth, and well fill the skull with tow, leaving some protruding to form a neck; also put some tow along the cheeks and in the mouth to replace the flesh and tongue. Return the skin to its original position, and properly shape the head by modelling the putty with the fingers from the outside. Eyes need not be put in. Now form a bag of chamois leather to fit inside the body, and finish as is shown by Fig 43.

CHAPTER IV.

ANIMALS' HORNED HEADS: POLISHING AND MOUNTING HORNS.

ANIMALS' horned heads are among the most favourite specimens of the taxidermist's art. The possibility of making a good job of any head depends greatly on the length of neck skin that has been left.

Gamekeepers and others, who should know better, when dealing with a deer, frequently slit the skin up the throat. Then it is impossible to sew up the skin without showing an ugly line of stitches in the most prominent part. Another fault is, that even those who are anxious to send the specimen correctly leave a long piece of skin attached to the back of the head only, whereas a little thought might have convinced them that not only must the neck skin be long at the back, but the front should be even longer.

Upon receiving the head, unless it can be taken in hand at once, it is much safer to place it without delay in a pail of strong brine. Unless this simple precaution be taken, it will most likely be found that the hair will "slide" when the work is begun, and then it will be impossible to make a satisfactory piece of work of it.

When about to begin, take out the head, wash it in clean water to remove the salt, and as it is presumed that a deer's head is to be mounted, at the same time with soap and water scrub and clean the antlers or horns.

The necessary tools and materials are: Knife, strong scissors, tenon saw, chisel, mallet, awls, hammer, long screws or French nails, a piece of 1-in. or $1\frac{1}{2}$-in. deal, putty, tow, thread, eyes, cardboard or sheet zinc or copper, peat, and plaster-of-paris.

Commence with pencil and paper. Make a few rough sketches, and on them place the measurements. Notice the shape and size of the nostrils, the formation of the lips, and the way in which the eyelids lie when the eye is open. It is mainly, if not altogether, upon these points that the character of the animal depends, and it is upon these points that so many so-called naturalists fail, for a sheep, goat,

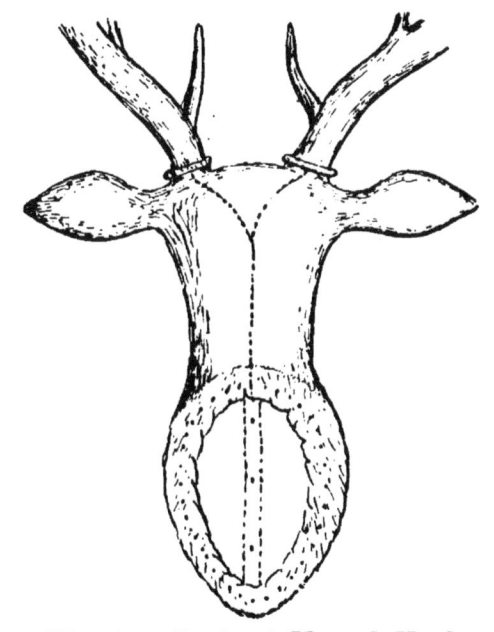

Fig. 44.—Back of Horned Head.

or deer, although possessing so many characteristics in common, has each its own peculiarities, and to miss these special points and treat them all the same is to perpetrate some of the glaring mistakes which have brought on taxidermy the ridicule of those who are real naturalists.

The head is placed with its back towards the operator, and cut midway up the back to within 2 in. of the base of the antlers, and from this point take two other cuts to the antlers, and cut up the back of these (see Fig. 44). Some carry this cut up to a point midway between the antlers, and then make a cross cut to the antlers, forming in this way a long-legged T, but this is not nearly so good as the method indicated in Fig. 44, where the cuts form a Y with a long leg.

Lifting up one of these pieces of skin, quickly skin along until stopped by a piece of flesh, which appears to project outwards from the head—this is, of course, the ear—and at once cut well into the flesh so as to sever the ear quite close to the skull. This leaves a lot of flesh inside the ear; but do not mind this, as it can be attended to later. Repeating this on the other side, the antlers may be reached, but here caution is necessary. The skin should be removed from the antler without leaving a particle of hair behind. This is one test of a good hand. But this skin is so intimately attached that it cannot be got to move very easily, so proceed to work by a kind of digging action, more difficult to describe than perform. However, dig the knife in at the burr of the antlers and gradually work it round by digging, so as to separate the hair from the antler. By merely cutting round with the knife instead of digging, probably some small pieces of skin and hair will be left attached.

Rapidly skin along until the eyes are reached, where great care is required because the eyelids have to be split, and this is most easily accomplished by placing the left forefinger inside the eyelid and feeling, as it were, how the edge of the knife is going, directing it with gentle movements, and making the cuts of little more than hair breadths. When an inch has been done a stop must be made at a dark line, for this is the junction of the internal and external skins, and from this part the eyelashes proceed. Now the eyelid is like an empty pocket turned inside out. Cut this loose, close to the eye. The use of this pocket will be seen shortly.

Leading from the corner of the eye nearest the nose will be found a hollow channel running downwards towards the nose. This is the lachrymal sinus or tear channel. Cut well into this, rather than towards the skin, or daylight will certainly be shown, especially towards the lowest part, and this is not desired. Before this, however, the inner angle of the skin of the mouth will be met, but as this is large, thick, and roomy, no difficulty will be found in splitting this from the teeth to the edge of the lips. It will be found advantageous to cut away a good part of the return of this skin, namely the "prickly" or papillated part that lies along the cheek inside the mouth. Rapidly pass on to the nose, and, as there is plenty of room, this will not be difficult. It is quicker and easier to skin if the cartilage of the nose is cut through. Take care that plenty of the mucous membrane, or skin inside the nostrils, is left.

The head has now been skinned, and the internal and external skins of the eyelids, the lips, and the nostrils have been separated to their tips.

Now the ears must receive attention. They must be split as near to the tips as possible, but if the worker goes to the very edge he is likely to cut the skin, which at the edge is very thin indeed. The fingers alone can do most of this, the knife being called into play only to cut through the connecting strings or fibres as they are found impeding progress. Thus the ear is turned inside out, and formed into a large pocket. The cartilage is to be left, but all the adhering flesh should next be removed. A few rough sketches and measurements may be made of the skinned head. Note that the cheeks are not protruding like hemispheres, but lying nearly flat, with an almost imperceptible swelling outwards, and filling up all the space between the jaws, coming nearly, but not quite, flush with the bony ridge under the eye (the orbital ridge or process).

There are two ways of proceeding now: 1. To

remove the skin completely from the head by cutting the skin from the teeth. The skin is then dressed with a preservative of some kind, or plunged into brine while the skull is next operated upon. This method has many advantages, and is best in the case of a large head, where the skull cleaning is likely to be a long affair, for it can then be boiled and got beautifully clean and free from flesh and fat, while the skin is being penetrated by the preservative. But the subsequent arrangement of the mouth is perhaps not quite so easy in all respects; therefore, for a first trial, the adoption of the second method is recommended. 2. The second method is to leave the skin joined to the head.

The skull may be cleaned now. By cutting downwards along the orbital process and then keeping along the flat bone underneath, it is quite possible to take away the cheek in one huge piece. By cutting down at the centre of the back of the skull and scraping downwards, as it were, towards the ear, most likely nearly all the flesh in this part will come away in a piece. Now attend to the eye. By cutting along the edge of the orbit, the whole of the eye, fat, etc., can be gently pushed inwards from the bone, showing how loosely attached they are. Then with a knife to cut through the connecting nerves, fibres, etc., and a steel or other lever to force or lift the whole upwards, the whole contents of the orbit may be brought away in a piece. By turning the head so that the lower jaw is uppermost, and cutting along the inside of the jaw, grazing the bone all along, the tongue and most of the adhering flesh will come away in a piece. Thus most of the flesh, etc., has been cleared from the skull in seven large pieces, viz., two cheeks, two eyes, two round the ears, and the tongue. With the saw make two sloping cuts into the floor of the skull, letting the cuts enter as near the sides as the jaws will allow, and the termination of the triangular prism thus formed will be in the hole at the back through which the spinal cord proceeds. With the chisel, cut down through the palate between the eyes, and the whole of the bone will come away in a piece, leaving exposed the base of the brain. With a little care, it is easy to separate the skin surrounding the brain from that lining the inside of the skull, for the two are quite distinct, and then the brain will come away unbroken. This is far less messy and disgusting than using a brain spoon and bringing away the brain in small quantities.

Look over the whole, removing any piece of

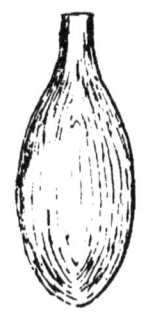

Fig. 45.　　　　　　　　　Fig. 46.
Turned Wood for Ear Block.

flesh which has been omitted; some will be found round the articulations of the jaws. The thick skin inside the skull should come away; the interior of the nose should also be cleaned and scraped; part of the papillated mucous membrane lying along the molar teeth may well be removed now, if not done previously.

Remove any bits of flesh, skin, etc., adhering to the skin; in fact, in order to model a head properly, it is necessary to thin the skin all over. The whole of the skin must be preserved, and for this purpose there is no better preparation than Browne's preservative, made by mixing together 1 part of saltpetre and 4 parts of burnt alum. This must be well rubbed on in every part of the skin; the hair will slide at any part that is missed. This mixture is very much quicker in its action, as well as more thorough, when made into a paste with water. Well cover every particle of the inside of the skin, being careful not to omit the eyes and ears. Well dress the

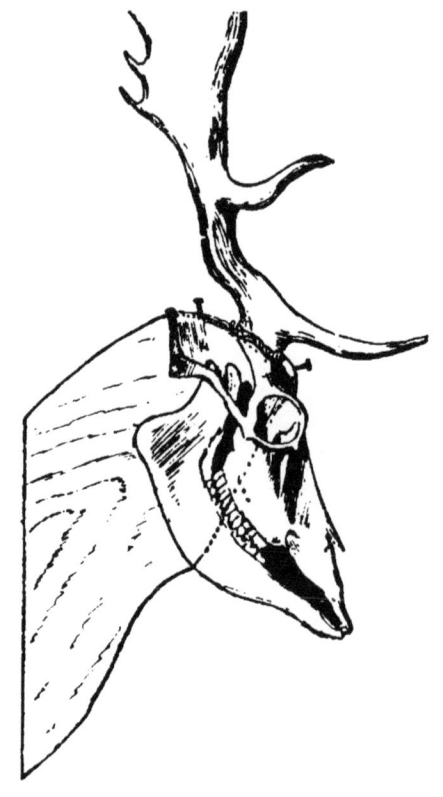

Fig. 47.—Skull with Centre Board for Modelled Neck.

bone and leave it for a time, twenty-four hours if possible, for the preservative to penetrate. During this time it will be advisable to procure a turned piece of wood shaped like Fig. 45. This, when sawn down the centre, will give two pieces of the shape of Fig. 46. On these pieces the ears are blocked, and down the centre of the flat surface of each about half a dozen or more tacks may be driven in to support the threads used in binding the ear to the block. Procure also some putty and a piece of cardboard. Out of the cardboard cut a piece of the same shape and size as the cartilage of the ear. Many use thin sheet zinc or copper for this purpose.

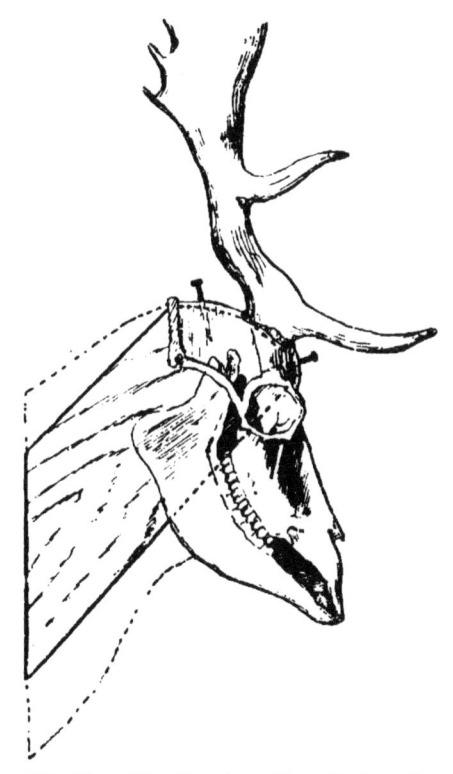

Fig. 48.—Skull with Centre Board for Loose Neck.

The second part of the work, namely modelling, may be begun now. First cut a piece of 1½-in. deal upon which to fix the skull. The length of this will depend upon the length of the neck skin attached to the head, and this should have been determined before the work began. By referring to Figs. 47 and 48 it will be seen that there are two shapes of these supports or centre boards. Whichever form is used, the skull must be firmly fixed to this support by long screws or French nails passing through holes previously drilled in the skull. These nails will be seen partly driven in in Figs 47 and 48. Keep the jaws fixed rigidly together by means of copper wire.

Having fixed the skull firmly, proceed to replace the larger masses of flesh by pieces of peat, roughly cut to shape, which may be attached by nails, wire, twine, etc. Peat is not absolutely necessary; paper, crumpled up and well rammed together, or tow rolled up into balls, may be used. Whatever material is used, it must be securely attached. One large

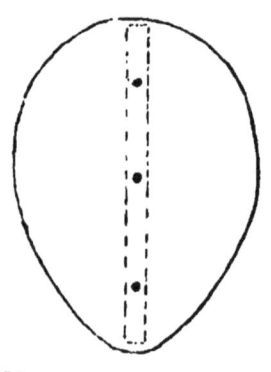

Fig. 49.—Neck Board for Horned Head.

piece will replace the tongue, two others will form the cheeks, two others will partially fill the orbits, etc. Leaving this for a time, mix some plaster-of-paris by sprinkling the plaster into the water and stirring until a rather thick cream is formed. With this the whole head is quickly covered wherever any flesh has been removed, gently but quickly modelling it into shape with a flat knife. Properly done, this will set very quickly indeed, so that speed is essential; but it may even then be brought into shape by the use of a rasp or knife. See that plenty of plaster goes down into the skull to help to fix the wood support or centre board.

If the method shown by Fig. 47, p. 74, were chosen, the neck board (Fig. 49) would have to be cut out first; then the size of this, its length, as well as the angle at which the head is to hang, should have been determined by the length of the neck skin before operations were commenced. Attach this neck board to the centre board by three long screws as

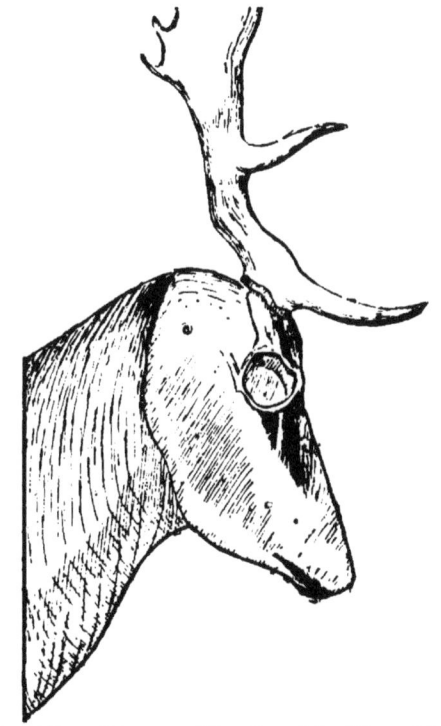

Fig. 50.—Plaster Head with Tow Neck.

shown in Fig. 49, where the dotted lines represent the position of the centre board.

Now proceed to bind tow, peat, shavings, wood-wool, or even paper, to form an artificial neck, making it full on the sides and gradually tapering, being careful to form all the depressions or swellings of the various muscles, not bringing everything to a dead level of uniform plumpness (see Fig. 50). Many of the more advanced taxidermists now cover the whole of the neck with plaster or modelling clay, giving the final touches with knives, rasps, modelling tools, etc., reproducing, as far as possible, every muscle. This, of course, requires a good knowledge of anatomy, which the beginner is not likely to possess; but good work can be done without this latter modelling.

Gently work the shapes cut out of cardboard, zinc, or copper, into the ears. Some flesh was removed from the bases of the ears, and this is replaced by putty. Take more putty, and place a layer inside the pockets of the lips and eyelids, also well pad the nose with the same. Now draw the skin over the model, taking care to get the inner angles of the eyehole correctly upon its proper part of the orbit, and at once drive in a fine tack or brad, or steel pin, to keep this in position, for if this is wrong, everything else will be wrong. Then press the tear track under the projecting ridge of bone, and drive in another pin at its deepest and furthest end. Now get the skin into position round the antlers more by gentle persuasion than by absolute force. Drive in one or two steel points through the skin into the bone close to the burrs, and proceed to sew this up, using the stitch illustrated by Fig. 18, p. 28. Continue down one arm of the Y, then leave off here, and with another piece of thread sew up the skin round the base of the other antler; carry the stitches down the other arm of the Y and tie the two threads together.

Be sure that the bases of the ears are well filled with putty, and that the ears stand out at equal angles.

If the centre board shown by Fig. 48, p. 75, is used, then the loose method of stuffing for the neck must be adopted. The neck board, as seen in Fig. 49, p. 76, is an egg-shaped piece of wood, cut from $\frac{3}{4}$-in. or 1-in. deal. The neck is stuffed by ramming in with the stuffing-iron (Figs. 11 and 12, p. 14) some pieces of tow, stitching downwards a couple of inches at a time, and making sure as the stuffing proceeds that the neck is well formed, nicely rounded at the top, and narrower towards the throat. On arriving at the neck board, the end of the skin must be forcibly drawn over and secured with tacks driven in at the back (Fig. 51). Then temporarily fasten it to a rough mount in order to hang it, when it is finished, out of the way to dry.

The lips and nose must be nicely modelled. The

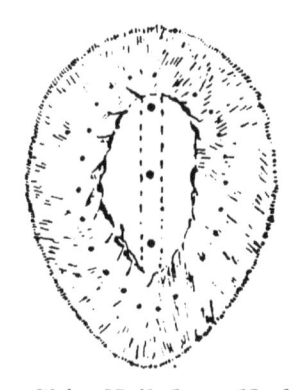

Fig. 51.—Skin Nailed on Neck Board.

weight of the putty in the pocket of the lower lip will have a tendency to cause this to droop, and doubtless too much of the mucous membrane of the upper lip is shown. The nose, too, is all out of shape. The notes and sketches taken before the skinning began now have their value. By stroking from the forehead downwards to the tip of the nose, the putty is forced downwards, lengthening the nose. The upper angles of the nostrils will require pinching in a little, making this part slightly narrower. The inside skin of the nose can be put into place with a penholder, and the lower angles also arranged by this means.

The rest of the work is difficult to describe, but

is very easy to do. Having got the nose correct, gently press the upper lip downwards with the finger, and the putty will go down, making this lip right. The lower lip requires pressing up from the chin, when the putty will go upwards, but would not keep there because of its weight and the contraction of the skin in drying. Therefore it is usual to keep the lips in position by stitching them together or by fine steel points driven into them. The latter method is to be preferred. Nothing now requires attention but the eyes. Fill in the orbits with putty, put in the artificial eye, noticing how the iris is arranged, then

Fig. 52.   Fig. 53.

Figs. 52 and 53.—Ear, Blocked and Bound.

gently draw over the lids and, with the awl, model in the depressions above and below the eyes. Now put an ear block (Fig. 46, p. 73) into each ear and bind it round with threads, allowing the threads to rest upon the tacks driven in the flat surfaces (Figs. 52 and 53), when they cannot become disarranged; see the finished head, Fig. 54.

Now the head on its temporary shield may be hung up out of the way to dry, a process which will take some weeks. During this time may be made the permanent mount or shield, some suitable designs for which are shown by Figs. 55 to 61, pp. 82 and 83.

To make these shields, double a piece of paper, draw half the shield, and then cut out through both pieces of the paper. Flatten out the paper, and mark round on the wood with a pencil. Then cut out with a fine saw, and, if desired, run a moulding on the edges. Across the centre of Figs. 56 and 57, p. 82, sections

Fig. 54.—Finished Horned Head.

are drawn showing how the edges may be finished. Oak, beech, walnut, and mahogany are perhaps the best woods. They must be well finished with plane and glasspaper and French polished. White woods stained and varnished should not be used, as they are apt to look trashy and spoil the appearance of an otherwise good piece of work. A hardwood shield,

F

stained black and then polished, looks well behind a light coloured head. Dull-polished ebony or

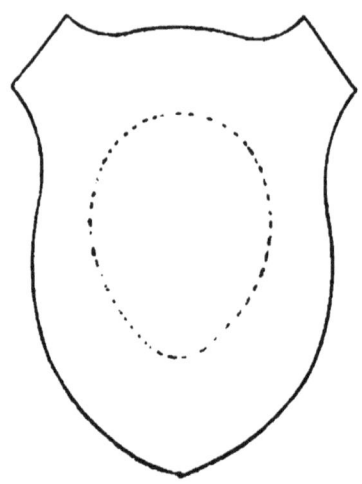

Fig. 55.—Shield Mount showing position of Neck Board.

ebonised wood is rather too gloomy for ordinary purposes, though often used.

The finishing touch is given when the head is

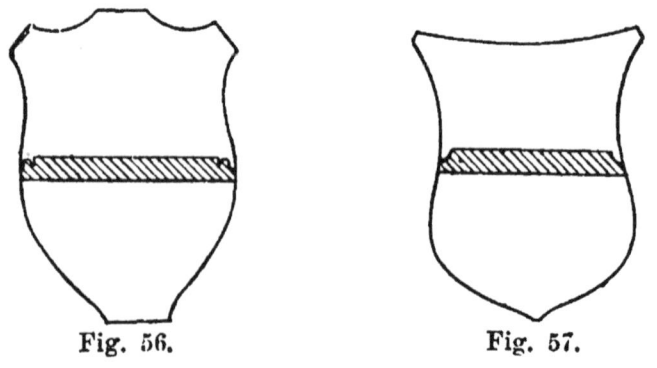

Fig. 56.   Fig. 57.

Shield Mounts.

dry. This consists in colouring the edge of the eyelids and the nose. Brunswick black is generally used; but a casual examination of an animal's nose will show that very few are black, and that still fewer are all of one hue. In most cases there are several shades, browns predominating, and these should be matched as nearly as possible.

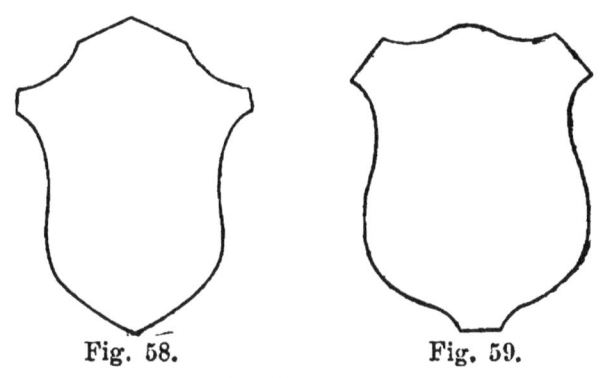

Fig. 58.   Fig. 59.
Shield Mounts.

As all uncased specimens are liable to the attacks of moths, or rather their larvæ, it is advisable, at least once a year, to take them down, brush them well to remove the dust, and then cover them with turpentine. When this has dried they may be re-

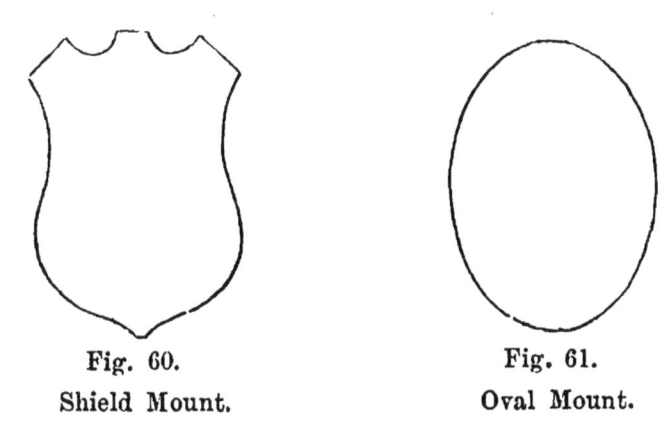

Fig. 60.   Fig. 61.
Shield Mount.   Oval Mount.

placed, and will well repay the small trouble entailed by enduring far longer than if neglected.

A pair of stag's antlers may be cleaned and mounted in the following way.

Well wash and scrub the antlers with warm water and soap. Thoroughly dry them with a cloth or towel, then give another smart rubbing with a perfectly dry cloth to remove some of the dulness from the sharp edges and prominences. Fig. 62 shows how, by cutting a piece off the back of the antler, it may be fixed to the mount by means of a screw passing through a hole previously drilled in the antler. Fig. 63 shows an artificial forehead of wood, with short processes upon which the antlers rest, being fixed from the back by a long screw. Another method is to drill a large hole lengthways into the antler from the base, and in this hole to place a

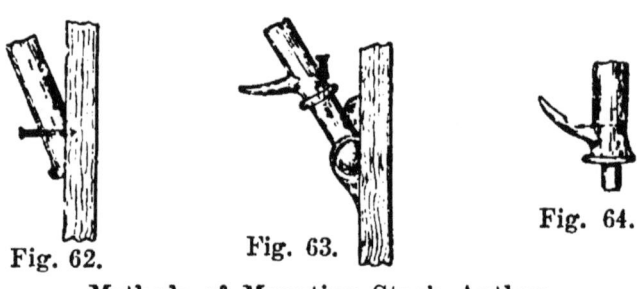

Fig. 62.   Fig. 63.   Fig. 64.

Methods of Mounting Stag's Antlers.

dowel (see Fig. 64), by means of which the antler may be fixed as in Figs. 62 or 63. Designs of suitable shields or mounts are shown by Figs. 55 to 61.

Deers' antlers may be mounted to form hat-pegs in a very simple manner.

Procure a piece of hard wood, oak for preference, and cut it into a heart-shaped shield. After well dressing the surface, and either chamfering or moulding the edges, polish the whole. With an ordinary tenon saw begin about an inch behind the antlers and cut the bone in a slanting direction towards the forehead, causing the saw to come out about 3 in. in front of the antlers. Thus the antlers attached to the forehead will have been detached from the rest of the skull, and when the forehead is placed in position upon the shield, each antler should be the same distance from the shield. It is therefore necessary to see that the same amount of bone is left on each side. Now fasten the antlers to the shield by driving in a couple of long screws through the forehead and into the shield. A brass plate, similar to those used for holding overmantels and pier-glasses, may be fixed at the back of the shield by which to support it.

Deers' horns and ox horns are not polished in the same way. The horns in the two cases are of different materials, the animals producing them being on this account placed by naturalists in separate families. Bullocks' horns are of true horn, and are detachable from the bony core on which they grow as a sort of hardened skin. Deers' horns are solid throughout, and grow direct from the skull, to which they are rooted. The most successful way to clean a pair of antlers is to wash them well with soap and water and a scrubbing brush, and then let them dry. The surface can then be further scrubbed with a hard clean brush till a gloss appears on the more prominent parts. The tips of the prongs can be scraped with pieces of newly-broken glass till the whiter part underneath appears. The appearance thus imparted is very good if the grade from white at the tip to dark brown is made gradual by careful scraping. A further gloss can be given by touching up the tips and more prominent parts with a thin solution of bleached shellac dissolved in spirit of wine and applied with a camel-hair brush. Some varnish the whole surface of the antlers with shellac solution, but in the opinion of others this does not look so well as when parts only are glossy and the general surface left dull.

Deers' horns and horns of the same nature can also be polished in the following way. Remove all the rough outer part with a rasp, followed by a file. Then well scrape with a knife, steel scraper, or side of a steel chisel to remove all file marks. Then glasspaper off with various sizes of glasspaper, finishing off with the finest. Now carefully remove any particles of dust, and repeat this dusting between every two of the subsequent operations. To polish the horns, apply, by means of a rag dipped in linseed oil, some of the horn dust saved during the previous processes, and rub

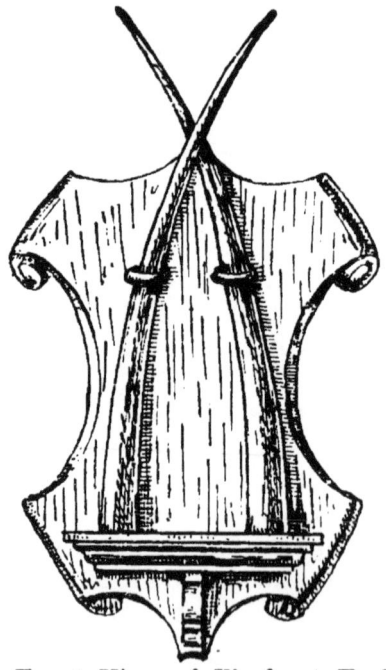

Fig. 65.—Front View of Elephant Tusk Mount.

smartly. Next apply some putty-powder or rottenstone by means of a flannel damped in water, and again use plenty of rubbing. Whiting is next employed by the aid of a rag damped in vinegar. Follow this with a chamois leather and a little oil, then with a clean dry leather, and finish off with a sharp rubbing with the bare palm.

Elephants' tusks are polished in exactly the same manner as described above for horns. Whiting is made into a cream with water, vinegar, or methylated spirit, and applied with a nail-brush. After briskly rubbing till all surface marks have been removed, it is again rubbed with a brush and water. It is then dried with a soft cloth and finally rubbed with a brush having just a drop of oil upon it. Another method is as follows. Obtain a piece of

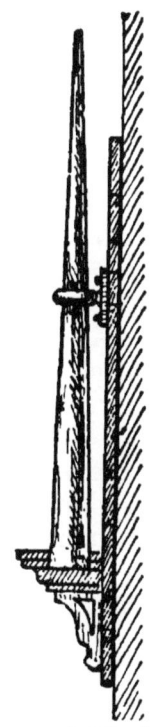

Fig. 66.—Side View of Elephant Tusk Mount.

wood, say 18 in. by 2 in. by ½ in., and cover one side with felt or thick cloth. The other side is to be covered with chamois, buff, or wash leather. In fastening these, let the nails enter the ends of the boards, then there will be no risk of scratching the work. A razor strop may be taken as a model, the leather, etc., being fastened near the handle first, then turned back and fastened by nails entering the end. The moistened whiting is applied to the cloth-covered side and rubbed on the tusk briskly, but no flats should be formed. The work is then dried with a cloth, and finally polished by means of dry whiting applied with the leather side of the board.

Figs. 65 and 66, pp. 86 and 87, show a design for a mount suitable for a pair of tusks. The shield-shaped board should be 1 in. thick, of oak, mahogany, or pitch pine, chamfered at the sides and rounded at the corners, as in Fig. 65. To this should be fixed a piece of similar wood, about $3\frac{1}{2}$ in. thick, with the front and ends moulded as shown in section, Fig. 66. In the top of this two holes $1\frac{1}{2}$ in. deep should be drilled to receive the ends of the tusks. Fix two brass rings with back plates and screws, as shown in Figs. 65 and 66. The smaller ends of the tusks pass through these, and are thereby held in position.

When polishing African horns, steam them for a few hours, and then with an old razor carefully scrape them; or a piece of glass broken off clean will answer the purpose. Next get some of the finest glasspaper, and face them up, rubbing always with the curve of the horn. Follow up with putty-powder (oxide of tin) and water on a piece of thick cloth or blanket; next with putty-powder in a dry state. With the aid of a polishing lathe, a brilliant polish may be got with a soft leather buff and fine dry lime. The mounting of such horns very much depends upon their size and shape. They may be made into snuff- and tobacco-boxes by fitting with silver or electro-plated mounts, having for a base a polished oak or mahogany stand, furnished with four ball-shaped feet. Or, as already described, they could be mounted in pairs on a tablet, and fixed against the wall as an ornament. And, if not too large, they could be arranged in the form of a hat- and coat-stand for the hall.

A ram's horn often is mounted to form the handle of a walking-stick. To do this wash the horn with strong soda-water, so as to remove all dirt and adherent matter. To polish it, scrape the roughness off with a broken glass or steel scraper, and further smooth it with the finest glasspaper. Next, colour by a penny packet of black dye. Or the horn may be left in boiling hot writing ink till black enough. To mount the horn on a stick, shape the stick's end with a knife, rasp, and coarse glasspaper till it fits the interior of the horn tightly. Then dip it into the dye or ink; and, when dry, cover it evenly all over the shaped end with cycle cement, holding it over a gas flame or near a fire, and spreading the cement about $\frac{1}{16}$ in. thick. Warm the interior of the horn and soften the cement till it begins to run; then insert the stick and hold it till cold. In half an hour or so scrape off superfluous cement. Reduce the horn and stick there to true circular section. A band of silver or other metal, fastened with three or four rivets, should hide the joint. Cut a round hole of the required size in a piece of tinplate; cut the tinplate in two, and use one half as a gauge. Wrap a piece of thin card of the proper width round the rounded part of the stick, which should, of course, be as long as the band is to be wide. Push a pin through where the ends overlap, unwrap the band, and shape it with scissors. Then cut out a piece of brass, silver, or other metal to the cardboard, and fasten it round the joints with rivets. The horn can be polished with whiting and water.

To polish a pair of ox horns, first remove all roughness from the horns by means of a spokeshave or rasp, followed by a scraper, a knife, the side of a chisel, a wood scraper, etc. Then go over them with sandpaper or glasspaper, using coarse paper first, then finer, and the finest last. Pumice powder should next be used, followed by the dust removed from the horn; these can be applied on a rag dipped in oil. Then apply putty powder in the same way, followed by whiting moistened with vinegar. Now use dry cloths, commencing with a coarse one and finishing with a soft one, or even tissue paper. Lastly, use the bare palm of the hand. In applying each of the above-mentioned substances plenty of "elbow grease" must be used, and the work must be very carefully dusted between successive stages to remove any trace of coarse grit. The use of a lathe with calico mops, etc., if procurable, will save time and labour and will give a better result.

To remove bone from an ox horn, place the whole in a moist, warm place—a manure heap, if available, will act splendidly. Bury the horn among the manure and leave it for a week or so, then take it out and try if the two parts can be separated. By fixing the butt of the horn in a vice, more force can be applied. Failing to separate them, bury them for another week. Now well wash the horn with water containing carbolic acid, to remove the rotting matter and to destroy the smell. Another method of removing the bone from an ox horn is to drill a hole in the bone and into it to turn a large coach bolt or similar screwed piece of iron. This, held in a vice if necessary, will form a handle to pull at. Leave the horn out of doors for a few days, or put it into a copper of hot water, till the core separates. The parting will be assisted by twisting and shaking the core by means of the handle. The core will eventually come out clean and leave nothing objectionable behind. These methods are suitable for many kinds of horns.

The cleaning and polishing of rams' horns, if these are dirty and have an unpleasant smell about them, is done after the core has been removed by one of the methods detailed in the above paragraph. Then boil the bony core and carefully remove all meatiness from it; painting with carbolic acid will also help to preserve it from decay. The horns proper may then be washed with hot water and soap and a scrubbing-brush to remove dirt, and then dried. Crinkled horns such as rams' had better not be scraped unless enough patience is possessed to go over all the ins and outs with a glass scraper and some fine glasspaper. To give a glossy appearance it is usual to varnish them with white shellac dissolved in spirit of wine, ½ oz. in 1 gill. This is applied with a camel-hair brush. Then the horns can be refixed on the cores with glue.

Buffalo horns are polished by rasping, scraping, and glasspapering, the polishing being carried onward with pumice- and rotten-stone until the surface is smooth and fairly polished; the horns may require bleaching if of a yellow colour, but any bleaching or dyeing should be done before the final polish is given. To bleach, use a weak solution of chloride of lime. Another method—exposure to the sun—is safe, but very slow. Experiment on a small scale, beginning with about half a teaspoonful of chloride to 2 oz. of water. Before dyeing the tips of the horns prepare a mash by boiling good bran in water for an hour. Strain off the liquor, and soak the tips in this for half a day or more; then dry well, and touch with the hands as little as possible. For a black dye, take 2 oz. of logwood chips, 1½ oz. of copperas, 1 qt. of water, and just a dash of China blue. Boil all together in an old iron pot. Apply hot in one or more coats. When dry, wipe over with vinegar in which has been steeped a handful of rusty nails or iron filings to the pint. This latter preparation fixes and intensifies the colour.

To mount a pair of buffalo horns, first obtain a piece of hard wood, oak for preference, sufficiently long to go some inches into each horn, leaving a space between the horns of at least 6 in.—the longer the horns the greater the space between them. Dress the wood with a plane, spokeshave, and rasp into a cylinder rather larger in diameter than the butts of the horns. Then shape each end to fit the horns. Now warm both the wood and horns, and fix them together with glue, cycle cement, etc., and finally drive a French nail through each horn (previously drilled) into the wood. A piece of black astrachan or dyed lambskin is finally used to cover the bare wood and the junctions of the horns. A couple of screw-rings fixed into the block will enable the horns to be suspended.

The taxidermist often requires to produce skeletons of animals, and there are two or three methods of effecting this; not one of them is very pleasant.

For such animals as horses and dogs, first take away the skin and the internal organs, and then with the knife remove the greater part of the flesh. Next place the bones in frequently changed water until the flesh has putrefied, and then either pick or wash it off. This, though very disgusting, is the method usually adopted. During the maceration, the connections or ligaments will give way, so that it may be advisable to tie or bind the bones with wires (copper preferred) before beginning the work. After the bones are cleaned, they must be permanently joined by brass or copper wires of sizes to suit the bones, holes being drilled for the purpose.

Another method of producing a skeleton is to boil the bones until the flesh can be picked off by the fingers, aided by blunt tools, bits of wood, etc. This is easiest done while the flesh is still hot. Another boiling will still further cleanse the bones, after which the skull should be placed in clean cold water, frequently changed, for a week or two. The bones may be placed on an anthill, or near a wasps' nest, or, if near a pond or the sea, immersion in the water will enable tadpoles, fish, etc., quickly to remove the flesh. To bleach, wash the bones in soap and water, using plenty of soda to free them from grease, etc. Then place them in a weak solution of chloride of lime in water, say 1 oz. to the pint, and proceed as under.

The simplest method of producing a skeleton, though liable to make the bones greasy-looking, is to boil the skull until all the flesh can be easily removed with pieces of blunt wood; but steaming the skull would be better if it could be arranged. The other method, by which the skull is macerated in cold water, and, when the flesh has putrefied, is afterwards scraped and scrubbed until clean, is very disgusting. Special bone-scrapers are used by professional osteologists, but for a single specimen a penknife would suffice. The dirt can be removed by well scrubbing with plenty of soap and soda, combined with the scraping; and if, after soaking in the chloride of lime solution, the result is not satisfactory, wet the skull every morning and evening, and leave it exposed to the sun and wind until bleached. Two things should be remembered—every particle of flesh, skin, etc., must be removed; and the scraping having been commenced must be finished, or the skull placed back in the water.

Perhaps the best way of bleaching bones is by means of hydrogen peroxide. The bones are placed in a pot with water, and hydrogen peroxide and strong ammonia are added while the pot is gently heated; the bones are then removed and allowed to dry in the sun. This is an expensive process. For common purposes the bones may be bleached by steeping in dilute nitric acid or chloride of lime, with thorough washing in water afterwards. Previous to any bleaching operations the bones should be boiled for some time with soda and water, to remove the grease.

Bone is softened by placing it in a kettle together with ashes and about one peck of lime to one barrel of bones. This is covered with water and boiled as long as required.

CHAPTER V.

SKINNING, STUFFING, AND CASTING FISH.

THE skinning and mounting of fish are attended with far greater difficulty than are the skinning and mounting of either birds or mammals, for, though the skin is tough enough in most parts to render the fear of rupture very remote, yet the danger of dislodging the scales, which cannot be replaced, is so great that the utmost care has to be taken. But if the skinning be performed without mishap the rest of the work is easily accomplished.

The most suitable fish for the beginner to take in hand first is a fair-sized perch, for the skin is tough, and the scales are small and tightly fixed. Before beginning to open it, place it with the better side downward, and get a piece of stoutish wire and bend it to the exact shape of the fish. It is well to be very careful over this, for it will afterwards be of the greatest possible use in affording an exact guide for the modelling, and will almost prevent the most common fault—making the fish too long and thin.

Fig. 67 represents the fish before it is opened, and Fig. 68 is the wire shape, in which A B and C D exactly correspond in size and curves to those parts of the fish between the head and the tail. Between A and C a wedge-shaped form is given to act as a support for the head, and at the apex a loop E is formed, the use of which will be seen shortly. The two free ends at B and D are now bent over to cross at F, midway between B and D. Hold them together with the flat-nosed pliers (see Fig. 7, page 12), and twist them together for some distance. Bend one end over, and leave it as shown by Fig. 68 at G. Pass the other end through the loop E, twist it back upon itself to correspond with the other wire G, and bend it to the angle shown, as at H. There is now an exact wire

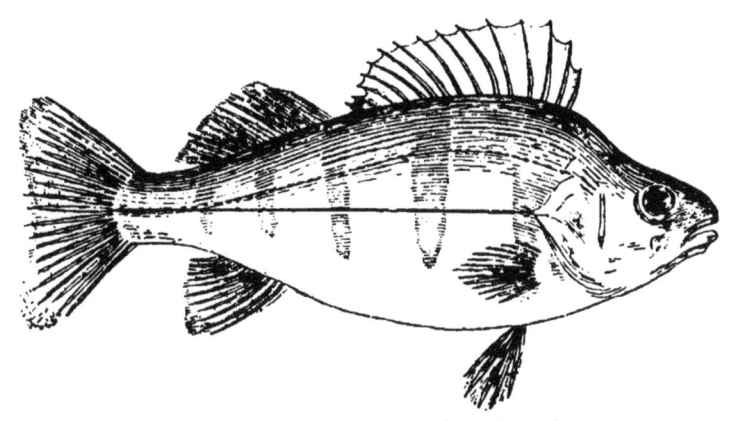

Fig. 67.—Perch Ready for Opening.

outline of the fish with a wedge-shaped support for the head, which is joined to the tail end by a central wire, the whole lying in the same plane, and from which project two wires at right angles for supporting the fish in the case. The shaping of the wire will not take even a beginner more than five minutes.

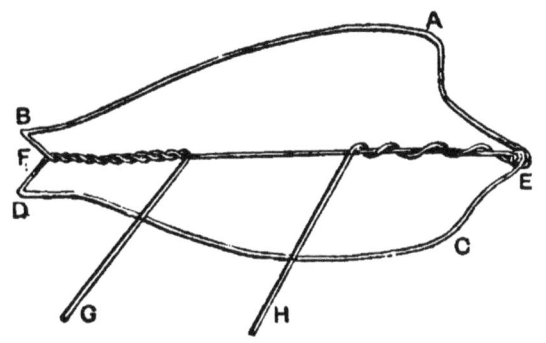

Fig. 68.—Wire Shape of Fish.

Place the wire shape out of the way, and begin with the skinning. Cover the better side of the fish with paper or muslin in order to keep the scales in place. This will most likely adhere by the natural mucus of the fish, but, if not, should be made to adhere with a little glycerine and gum water. Wrap the fins and tail in wet rags and tow to keep them moist, for if they get dry they will split. The fish should now be opened in a straight line along the worse side from the head to the tail, midway between the back and the belly. Some fish are marked with a line (the lateral line) which will serve as a guide. In the perch this line is too high, and is curved. Commence by cutting through the scapular arch—the bone under the gill cover—with the scissors, and then with either knife or scissors continue this cut to the tail; the cut is indicated by a straight line in Fig. 67. With the point of the knife lift up the upper edge of the skin, and hold it with the left finger and thumb, while the knife separates the skin from the flesh all along and up to the top of the back. A little sand is useful to dip the fingers in to prevent the skin slipping. Repeat with the lower side. When the fins are reached much more care will be required, for the skin here is very delicate. It is safer to leave some flesh on, and the bones rather long, for a rupture here would be very awkward. The skin near the vent is also very thin; therefore do not clear away too much before separating. One side is now quite clear, and, by working with the fingers alone, much of the underside may be separated from the flesh, especially along the back; but be careful, in passing the fingers down this, that they are not torn by the sharp edges of the bones left attached to the fins. Use the knife wherever it is possible, and, as soon as the fingers can be made to meet near the tail, slip the scissors in and cut through both flesh and bone, but leave plenty of flesh in. Now the work gets easier, and quick progress is made, the fingers alone separating the skin from the flesh along the back and part of the side. When the fins are reached the scissors are used.

The pectoral fin is the most awkward to manage. Cut through the backbone near the head, then through the gullet, and any flesh which may hold, and the body will come away in one piece. In the case of a larger fish it may be advisable to take the body away in sections. The skin now lies flat upon the table, and some flesh will be seen still attached to it along the lower side, at the tail and fins, and near the skull; also there may be a wedge-shaped piece between the lower jaw. First attend to the tail and clear the skin to the end of the bone. Plenty of patience will be needed. Scrape away the flesh, and cut the bone off short. Carefully scrape, not, by any means, cut, away the flesh near the fins, and shorten these bones. Assuming that all the rest is done, the head next needs attention. The gills are first removed by separating them at the top and bottom and pulling them away. Then, by opening the skull, on the under side, the brain is exposed for removal. Next, by removing a little more of the bone, the eyes may be taken out from the inside. The cheeks now require attention. By working from the outside, through the orbits, the flesh may be removed by the aid of the larger awl, the knife, and the fingers, using plenty of sand to give a grip. The wedge-shaped piece, running between the pectoral fins to a point beneath the jaw, is enclosed in a delicate silvery skin, and much care and patience must be exercised here. All the flesh has to be taken away. The tongue is best removed with any adjacent flesh, unless desired to be shown, when it will be necessary to cut from the outside and scrape out all the flesh, replacing this with putty and then sewing up. Now give another look all round, bearing in mind that any flesh which is not removed will ultimately shrivel up.

The preservatives recommended for birds and mammals (see pp. 16 and 17), are equally applicable to fish, but the stuffing material may be different.

Some use bran, others sawdust, or a mixture of bran and sawdust. Others use dry plaster-of-paris. It is difficult to say which is best. Tow alone is not a success, though sometimes used. Sawdust, with a sprinkling of carbolic powder, may be recommended.

Commence by filling the head with tow, and the cheeks, etc., with putty. Then place a good pad of putty round the tail, fins, and pectoral process (the wedge-shaped piece under the jaw). Insert the prepared wire stiffener (Fig. 68, p. 95), and fit it into shape, allowing it to lie as close to the skin as possible. Enough sawdust, bran, or dry plaster should now be put in to about half fill the skin. Begin to sew up at once, using a fine glover's needle. Drill two small holes through the scapular arch, pass the needle through both, and tie the thread. Then pass the needle through a hole drilled in the gill cover immediately above them, and then through each side of the skin alternately, far enough from the edges to prevent tearing, and continue this down to the first supporting wire, putting more sawdust in, and well pressing and ramming it towards the head.

Tie the thread firmly to the supporting wire, and leave off here and attend to the tail, making the first stitch at the tail, and carrying the stitches up to the second supporting wire, putting more sawdust in as progress is made, and pressing and ramming it well towards the tail. It is advisable to tie the thread to the second supporting wire, as then the stitches cannot slip. The ramming is most easily performed with a piece of wood or the end of a cedar pencil. Before continuing further it is well to make sure that the forepart and the tail end are well stuffed and rammed. Then gradually introduce more sawdust, pressing it well in all directions, and continuing the stitching an inch at a time. When all is firm and well filled, finish the stitching. Now obtain another piece of wood, larger in every direction than the fish; bore two holes at the same distance apart as the two supporting wires, pass the wires through and bend them over, and the fish will be found fastened to the board; turn over the board, when, of course, the show side of the fish is brought into view.

The fish is now noticed to be too flat, which is caused by the skin accommodating itself to the flat surface upon which it lay while the stuffing was done. To correct this, tap it into shape by gentle blows given with the handle of a table-knife or a piece of wood shaped like a small cricket bat. A shoemaker's hammer may be used, but great care and experience are required in using this, and, in the hands of a beginner, it would do more harm than good, as the blows would almost certainly be given with too much force. Before doing this shaping it would be well to draw a damp cloth over the skin, to remove sawdust, etc. The gill cover probably opens too much, which is easily corrected by placing a piece of cork between the nose and the board, in order to raise this part and therefore close the gill cover.

From the commencement of the skinning up to the present time the fins and tail should have been kept constantly damp, and it is now time to remove the wet rags, tow, etc., in which they were wrapped, and to set them into position. For this purpose nothing can be better than some pieces of sheet cork about $\frac{1}{8}$ in. thick. The fins are stretched and pinned between two pieces of cork which are kept in this position until the fins are quite dry. Directly the outer surface of the fish is dry, it will be found advantageous to give it a coat of quickly-drying spirit varnish in order to prevent the scales rising during the drying of the skin. The gill cover, if not quite close, should be bound down with cotton, wrapped round both board and fish; and this wrapping may also be done to any scales which have already risen. Nothing more is required until the fish is quite dry, when it will be found that it has lost all colour and assumed almost the appearance of leather.

The colour of a stuffed fish must be restored by coating with thin oil paints (using artists' tube colours) which must be so gradually run one into the other that no lines of separation can be seen. For this colouring, obtain a similar fish to the preserved one, and use this as a copy from which to colour the one in hand. It is impossible to go far wrong when nature is taken as a guide. The colouring of a dried fish is a delicate operation requiring a fair amount of artistic ability, which can be gained only by practice. Very little colour should be used, and it should be well thinned with turps and colourless varnish to represent wetness. The colours should be so applied as to leave neither streaks nor unnatural markings.

In the case of a jack or pike, as a rule, the irides are golden yellow; the back and front dark greenish brown, fading off on the sides to a dirty white, with perhaps a tinge of blue; oval spots vary from a white to a yellow or even brown; the belly is white. Others have the back of a greenish gold colour, shaded to a creamy white under the belly, with the lozenge-shaped spots yellowish, somewhat faint on the back, then bright on the sides and again fading towards the belly. The fins are brownish or yellowish, with deep purple edges and ribs and wavy bars. At spawning time the colours are much brighter.

In the roach the iris, lips, and fins are red (vermilion and carmine), the back greenish, in some specimens approaching black, and the sides and belly silvery. Silver paint should not be used on fish, as it has a tendency to darken with age. Practically, the same silvery effect can be obtained by the use of artists' tube colours—white with a very little blue for a golden fish colouring; try annatto or methyl orange amongst the coal-tar colours—the latter is a brilliant golden dye in a neutral or alkaline solution.

In the case of a trout, the colours vary, some being silvery with minute spots, and others nearly black with large spots. In some, again, the spots are jet black, while in others the black spot is surrounded by one or more rings of quite different colours. In one case, the nose and front of a trout's head were deep brown; the cheeks yellow with a greenish tinge; the pupil black with a red edge; the iris silvery with a black crescent border; the back grey with a tinge of green; the sides yellowish green; spots on the back, black, those on the sides being reddish surrounded by blue; pectoral fins fine light brown; the ventral fins red; the anal fin purple near the body, fading to yellowish grey; the tail deep greenish brown; adipous fin yellow, bordered with brown; dorsal fin grey, with purple spots. The most useful colours in painting a trout are black, white, reds (light red, vermilion, crimson), yellows (chrome, ochre), blues (Prussian, permanent), and browns (sepia, vandyke).

The eyes used are known as "flints," and are colourless. Before being used they require tinting and gilding. They are usually placed in with putty when the fish is dry, and just before colouring it, though for some reasons they are best inserted directly the fish is stuffed. If any of the fins should have split, they may be repaired with thin paper pasted on the back of the fin and then coloured.

The greatest objection to the above method of stuffing, and every other method of fish stuffing, is the shrivelling of parts of the head, especially above the eyes and round the mouth. This can be hidden by coating them with hot wax, and then colouring. This waxing is very simple, and should always be done.

Another method of stuffing is often employed. This consists in forming a body of tow, paper, etc., well pasted, and wrapped with cotton round a central wire. This is made to correspond as closely as possible in size with the original body. A pad of putty is now placed round each fin, and sometimes a layer is put all over the skin. The prepared body is inserted in the skin, placed accurately in position, and then sewn up.

A more accurate method than either of the above is to form a mould in plaster-of-paris of one-half of the fish. Then skin the fish, place the skin exactly in position upon the mould, and stuff with well-rammed sawdust, bran, or plaster. In this case the shape must be accurate.

It is impossible accurately to represent water

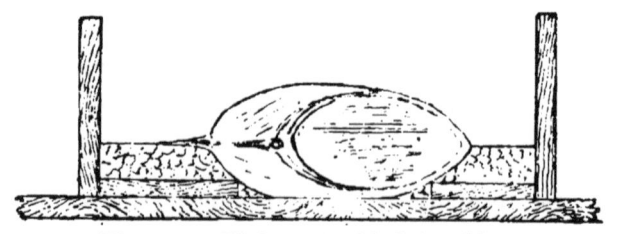

Fig. 69.—Fish embedded in Clay.

with the fish swimming in it, and it is best not to attempt it; therefore, leave the glass of the showcase uncoloured, and the back of the case simply tinted pale blue. The bottom of the case may be covered with sand, varnished to appear wet, and a few pebbles, rushes, etc., introduced. The two positions of fish which are most realistic are: (1) lying in a flat basket partly filled with straw, as though the fish had just been unpacked; and (2) lying on a grassy bank as though just caught.

Two cases most suitable for fish are mentioned in Chapter VIII., pp. 150 and 151.

A few hints upon fish casting and modelling may be of service, since fish casts are more in public favour at present owing to the unavoidable shrivelling of the soft parts of the head in the set up specimens. This shrivelling can readily and easily be hidden with wax, though very few taxidermists do this, preferring to leave the plump, pouting lips dried up and mummified rather than improve on the old-fashioned process.

First remove the natural mucus or slime from the fish by washing in dilute sulphuric acid or vinegar; then place it in the desired position upon a piece of wood, paper, or cardboard. Take some pieces of wood and place them round the fish to form four walls, one or two inches higher than the highest part of the fish. Get some small pieces of wood and pack them round the fish. Now put some well-tempered clay over the wood and round the fish

Fig. 70.—Clay-embedded Fish covered with Plaster.

until the lower half of the fish is quite hidden (see Fig. 69). The clay will thus form a support for the dorsal fins and tail, and if these will not keep the desired position, fine headless pins may be driven through the outer parts and into the clay; but these should be cut off so as not to project above the fins. With a broad flat knife, such as a putty knife, smooth the clay, because when finished this part forms a tablet upon which the fish rests. Now mix up the plaster, which should be the finest possible kind known as S. F., by sprinkling the plaster in the water and stirring well. Continue this sprinkling and stirring until it is of the consistency of cream. Give both fish and clay a good wetting with water, and then pour the plaster quickly but gently upon the fish. Enough should be mixed to cover the whole at once. More should then be mixed to cover this; and more after that, if wanted, until it stands, say, about an inch above the side of the fish (see Fig. 70, p. 103). Now leave all for a time, probably about half an hour will suffice. By the end of this time the plaster should be firm enough to enable the whole to be turned over and the fish to be taken out. Then there is a mould in which every mark and every scale has left its impression. Fig. 71 gives a section of the plaster mould, which should be well oiled or wetted, or have a good dressing of soap lather. Into this mould more plaster, mixed as before, is poured, and, when well set, it should be gently tapped till it separates from the mould, when a perfect impression of the fish will be seen lying upon a plaster slab (see Fig. 72).

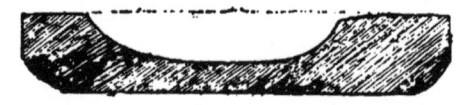

Fig. 71.—Section of Plaster Fish-mould.

The greatest drawbacks to plaster casts are their weight and brittleness. To avoid these, other substances are sometimes employed, the most satisfactory of which is paper, in some form or other. The easiest method, and in many respects the most satisfactory, is to take several sheets of tissue paper, paste them on both sides with good flour paste, apply them to the mould, and well press them in with a brush in order to get them into every depression; thus is made a kind of papier-mâché. These are followed by somewhat stouter sheets, until from five to eight sheets of paper have been employed. The whole is placed in a warm room until dry, when the model will readily leave the mould providing it was well oiled before the paper was applied. This model will weigh but a few ounces, and will be more satisfactory in every way than a plaster cast—one great gain being that paper will readily take colour whilst plaster will not, without preliminary treatment.

Another papier-mâché method is, briefly, to beat or mix paper and flour paste together and work them in a mortar, with or without pipeclay, until they form a homogeneous mass greatly resembling putty. Take about 1 oz. of tissue paper (say four sheets), 5 oz. of thick flour paste, and 1 oz. of powdered pipeclay. Beat the whole in a metal mortar to a pulp, and then work it a little at a time, in a similar manner to grinding paint, by a muller or spatula

Fig. 72.—Plaster Cast of Fish.

upon a stone or glass. Powdered colours may be added when mixing, and therefore save time when finally tinting. To use it, oil the mould, put a thin layer of the composition into the mould, and press well with the fingers to send it into every depression. Then place upon this a couple of layers of well-pasted strips or pieces of muslin, to form a backing to the papier-mâché, and allow the edges of the muslin to overlay about ½ in. This will prevent buckling. It should be allowed to dry slowly; probably a week will suffice. When dry, it will readily take colour, if a dressing of boiled oil be applied first.

Fish bones may be preserved in a white and semi-transparent state by many methods. By one as much fish as possible is removed in a raw state; then the bones are soaked in water, frequently changed, for about a week, or until the remnants of the fish still adhering can be taken off by sharpened pieces of wood. By another, the whole is boiled, and the fish removed while hot by any suitable instrument; knives are not suitable for this purpose. This boiling, if too prolonged, will cloud some of the bones. They are then boiled again and cleaned, left in cold water for a few days, and then dried in the sun. Lastly, they are covered with colourless varnish. If required to be semi-transparent bleaching must not be attempted. Most of the usual bleaching agents turn them white and cloudy.

Crabs are not boiled if it is desired to retain the natural colour. When dead, they must be carefully cut at the joints, and all the flesh must be removed. The joints of the legs will not need cutting, as the matter in them, if exposed to the air, will quickly dry; the claws should be quite emptied. The body of the crab should be opened, and the liver or cream removed. The thorax, where the legs are articulated, will be rather difficult. When all the parts are clean they must be set in their proper positions by means of glue or cement.

CHAPTER VI.

PRESERVING, CLEANING, AND DYEING SKINS.

ONE important branch of the taxidermist's art is the treatment of skins for making rugs, mats, etc., or, as in the case of skins from small animals, for making fur necklets, muffs, bags, etc. The many processes of treating skins for these purposes are quite distinct from ordinary leather tanning; though sometimes tanned hides are used for making rugs.

Tawing skins or white leather dressing is carried on in many countries and in many forms, but in all the methods there are three distinct operations: (1) Fleshing the skins; (2) tawing or preserving them; and (3) currying or softening the leather.

Fleshing consists in removing every particle of fat and flesh still remaining on the skin, and also the inner skin, which locks up, as it were, the true skin; but this thinning is frequently done after the tawing. In a commercial way this is generally accomplished by throwing the skin across a beam and shaving with a sharp two-handled knife; but later is described the method usually adopted by those who only occasionally have this work to do.

Tawing consists in immersing the skins in a liquid preservative, the skins being weighted or pressed down with strips of wood, so that they are quite covered with the liquid. They are left in this for about a day, but the exact duration depends upon the weather, and upon the thickness of the skin. If a piece of the skin be folded over and pinched, a white line will be left when the action of the preservative is completed. The preservatives are many. One of the best consists of a solution of 1 lb. alum and ¼ lb. salt in about 1 gal. of hot water. The action of this will probably

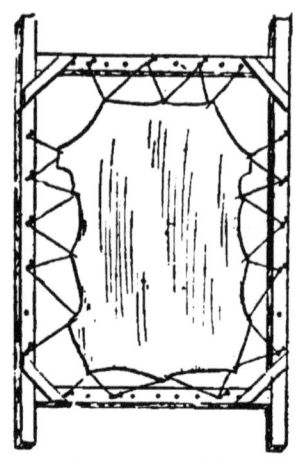

Fig. 73.—Skin-stretching Frame.

be found much quicker if the solution is used lukewarm.

Fig. 74.—Corner of Skin-stretching Frame.

Then the skins are stretched in every direction, being fixed by means of nails upon a door or the floor. Professional leather dressers use a frame of wood suited to the size of the skin, the four sides of the frame being bored for a number of holes. Into these holes pegs fit, and the skin is quickly stretched by cords going through the edges of the

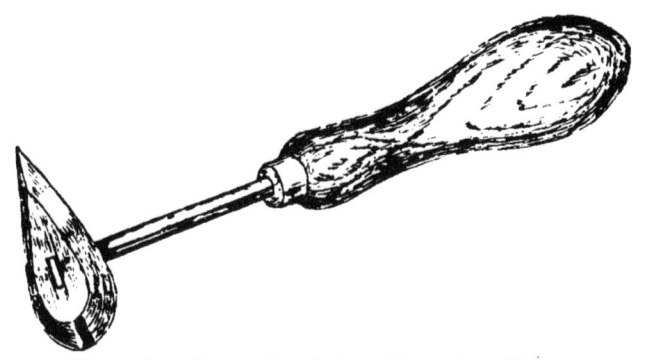

Fig. 75.—Shave-hook for Dressing Skins.

skin and round the pegs (see Fig. 73). Fig 74 shows how the corners of the frame are secured together. The skins thus stretched are allowed to dry.

Currying proper consists in working the skins over a sharp iron stake, but the same result may

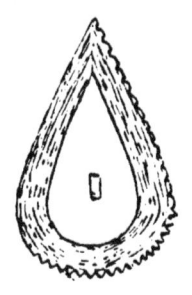

Fig. 76.—Serrated Blade of Shave-hook.

be accomplished by scraping the skin to remove the inner skin, which locks up the real skin in which the hair or fur is fixed. A very convenient tool is a plumber's shave-hook (Fig. 75), having one edge cut into teeth (Fig. 76) by means of a three-cornered saw-file; the teeth may be pointed in the round part, but chisel-shaped along the side. When the skin is stretched and nearly dry, it should be scraped in every part to tear off the hard pieces and to stretch open the fibres; this must be done well if the skin is to be soft. It should now be well rubbed between the knuckles, as in washing clothes. Of course, it should have been previously removed from the frame; and if an old table or

Fig. 77.—Furrier's Double-edged Knife.

bench, or even a box, is handy to throw the skin over, the scraper can be used more forcibly along the part lying over the edge.

In Fig. 77 is shown a double-edged flexible knife used by leather dressers and furriers for fleshing and reducing the thickness of the skins. Fig. 78 shows a curved stouter knife used in dressing the skins. This is frequently more curved than the sketch, being sometimes semi-circular. Fig. 79 is one form of a furrier's horse or beam. It is a

Fig. 78.—Furrier's Single-edged Knife.

scaffold pole fixed upon wooden supports, and upon this the skin is thrown while the knives are being used.

There are but one or two means, other than the paring-knife, of reducing the leather of fur skins. It is impossible to reduce the substance of the skins by the ordinary splitting machines as used for leather, owing to the presence of the hair or fur. But perhaps a block similar to that shown by Fig. 80

may be found useful, being both simple to make and inexpensive. Get a piece of wood about 2 in. thick and 10 in. square. Shape the top A as shown, and glue to it a sheet of coarse glass-paper C. There should be no sharp edges round the upper surface, or furrows and unevenness will result. To reduce the skin to the required substance, hold

Fig. 79.—Furrier's Horse or Beam.

the block firmly in a vice by a strong cross-piece B, fixed to the top by three screws, and work the flesh side of the skin over its surface, commencing at the thickest part. Examine it frequently to see that the parts operated upon are not reduced too much or otherwise injured. This will prove

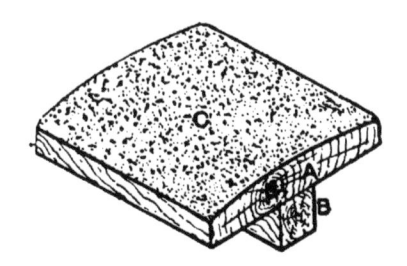

Fig. 80.—Sandpaper Block for Rubbing Skins.

not only a safe and efficient method, but a very expeditious one also, besides rendering the skin very soft and pliant.

The following are some of the many modifications of these processes. Supposing the skins are small (say rabbits') and fresh, they may be stretched upon a board and the edges secured with tacks. All the flesh and fat are now scraped away, and spirits of camphor well rubbed into the skin. A mixture of two parts of yellow soap and one part fine oatmeal is prepared and made into a rather thick paste, to which a small quantity of rum or other spirit is added. This is then spread upon the skin, and well rubbed in by means of a blunt, knife-shaped piece of wood. This process is repeated on several days, more of the mixture being added as required. The skins may then be finished off with dry oatmeal.

Colonel Park's method is to stretch the skins and nail them down to dry, and when enough are ready to thin them as usual, damping them with water previously. Then mix ½ pt. of salt, 1 oz. of best oil of vitriol, and 3 qt. of soft water, stirring with a stick. The solution should taste sharp, and may make the hands smart a little, but will do no harm; dipping the hands in cold water if necessary will relieve the smarting. When the skins have been in this for thirty minutes they may be taken out, squeezed, but not wrung, and then hung in the shade to dry.

Another method for fresh skins is to mix bran and soft water sufficient to cover the skins, but to let this stand for some hours before being used; immerse the skins, keeping them covered for twenty-four hours, and then take them out and carefully scrape off all flesh. To 1 gal. of hot water add 1 lb. of alum and ¼ lb. of salt. When these have dissolved and the mixture will bear the hand, immerse the skins and leave for twenty-four hours; take out, stretch, and dry in the shade, scrape well with the scraper, and give a good rubbing with the knuckles. Stir the liquor, and again immerse for twenty-four hours. Dry and hand-rub as before, and then put the skins for twenty-four hours into warm oatmeal and water, stirring occasionally. Dry in the shade, and when nearly dry rub till quite dry. This is a good method, but it may be found just as efficacious to mix the bran, alum, and salt with the hot water, thus saving one operation. In this form it will answer as well for dry skins as for fresh ones.

The furrier's method is to mix up a paste of alum, salt, flour, yolk of eggs, and water, and to work this into the skin until it has penetrated, when the remainder is scraped off and the skin is cleaned with bran or sawdust.

Another method is to steep and scour in a bath of alum, bran, and salt, and then in one of soap and soda to remove the fat; finish by thoroughly washing and drying.

Another method consists in using Browne's skin preservative, and to follow this by the usual currying. The composition of this preservative is given on page 73.

A new method, an American one, of preserving the skins of small animals for the sake of the fur is to wash the skins, freed from flesh and fat, with a strong lye of wood ashes, till the gluten is destroyed, but not prolonging the washing till the fibre is eaten away. Sperm oil is applied, and the skin is softened by rubbing equally all over it. In this way a squirrel-sized skin can be dressed in ten minutes, a rabbit-sized skin in fifteen minutes, and a calf skin in thirty minutes.

The uncombined oil in the skins must be removed. Some skins are very fat, especially those of dogs; but the excess of fat may be removed by washing in a solution of potash, or in a bath of soap and soda, or they may be scrubbed with a hard brush and hot soft water, during which a mixture of two parts by weight of salts of tartar and one part of ammonia may be sprinkled on.

Hunters abroad are sometimes anxious to know how to treat skins just separated from the animal; these skins should be "fleshed," laid down upon the ground and well rubbed with a paste of Browne's skin preservative (see p. 73) and a little water. Especial care should be taken with the eyes, nose, and ears, otherwise the hair may "slide" at these parts later on. The skin should then be folded, and the dressing repeated next day; then it should be dried in the sun and air. If convenient, it is best to stretch the skin upon a frame before applying the preservative, and keep it so till dry. Failing this, it must be stretched by pegging it to the ground. It is now ready to be packed away —in the flat is best, but that cannot always be done.

A skin that is to be dressed must be damped and shaved either with a currier's sharp-handled knife, or, as a makeshift, with a spoke-shave. Curriers would use a beam or "horse" when doing this, but the edge of a table will answer. When nearly dry the skin should be folded with the hair inside and the edges secured with a few stitches here and there, say a foot apart; this is to protect the hair. Cover the skin with lard, using about 3 lb. for a leopard's skin; then rub the skin so as to force the grease in. The hands are poor tools for this. A professional would put the greased skin into a tub and tread the grease in with his naked feet, but probably many persons would prefer to put it into a tub and use a washerwoman's dolly. Whichever method—feet, hands, or "dolly pegs"—is used, the grease must be made to penetrate the skin. Now cut the stitches, and, if necessary, further shave the skin, after which proceed with the cleaning of the fur. This is accomplished by rubbing sawdust containing no resin into the fur; mahogany dust from a veneer mill is best. When thoroughly well rubbed, shake and beat with light canes till the sawdust is all out, when the full beauty of the skin will be seen.

To those who want "skins as soft as chamois leather," it will be sufficient to state that up to the present no powder or solution has been found which will render the skins soft and pliable without further labour. This softness can only be obtained by a vast amount of patience and care being bestowed over the currying. It is the constant scraping and rubbing during the latter part of the drying that makes the skin pliable, and unless this is done thoroughly well the result will not be exactly satisfactory.

Following will be found a number of miscellaneous notes on the treatment of skins.

The grease in skins can be killed before applying a preservative by placing them in a mixture of bran and soft water, and allowing them to remain covered for twenty-four hours. This mixture should be prepared some hours before being used, as it acts better if it is in a state of fermentation. If preferred, the alum, bran, and salt may be made into a bath with water, and in it the skins may be placed, thus doing two operations in one.

To clean a badger skin, the white hair about the head of which is a dirty earth colour, place the skin upon the table, hair upwards, and have ready a basin of warm water, soap, sponge, and towel. Now wash the head, using no more water than is necessary; do not allow water to get upon the underside. Then soak out all the water the sponge will take, and finish the drying with the cloth or towel. Any stains that still remain would require to be bleached out by a rather severe process.

The cleaning of a white sheepskin can be accomplished with soap and water. Dissolve 1 lb. of. soap in 2 qt. of boiling water—rain water if possible. Put half of this in a tub with 4 qt. of cold rain water, and rub the sheepskin with the suds till they will not extract further dirt. Then use the other quart, diluted as before, to get the rest of the dirt out. Passing the sheepskin through a roller wringer will help matters considerably.

Rinse very thoroughly in warmed rain water, and pass through a roller wringer. Dry in the sun, the flesh side being exposed. Shake, and alter the position of hanging frequently as the drying proceeds. A little washing blue added to the last rinsing water will make the wool whiter.

In the case of the skin covering a mounted sheep's head, loose dirt may be removed by a thorough brushing; then wash it with soft flannel, warm water and white soap, a little laundry blue added to the final water being an improvement. Dry it with a sponge or flannel, followed by cloths or towels, and place it in the sun, wind, or a warm room to dry.

Of the many methods of cleaning a tiger's skin five are here given. (1) Moisten bran with hot water and well rub it into the fur with a piece of clean flannel. Finish by well rubbing in fresh dry bran with a clean dry flannel. (2) Rub damp (not wet) whiting well into the fur so that it goes down to the actual skin. Leave it till next day, when the whiting, which in the meantime has dried, should be well rubbed, then removed by shaking and brushing with an ordinary clothes-brush. Place the skin over the back of a chair, and well brush along the parting thus made, blowing away the dust and whiting at the same time. To brighten up the colours, benzoline should be applied by means of a clothes-brush, which should be passed lightly in the way of the fur, not against the fur. (3) Heat in an oven a mixture of equal parts of flour and powdered salt, and while hot thoroughly rub it into the fur. When the whole has been dressed, shake and brush out the mixture as described above. (4) To wash the skin, cut up a bar of soap and dissolve it in about 2 gal. of boiling water. Place the skin upon a table and wet the whole fur with the solution. A gentle rubbing with the hands will loosen most of the dirt. Now dilute about 2 qt. of the solution with 2 gal. of warm water, and continue the washing, the skin still lying upon the table. When the skin in quite clean, remove the soap with plenty of clean water. Then dry it by means of a clean sponge, followed by clean cloths. In this way little of the actual skin will become wet. Now hang it in the shade, and frequently take it down and shake it well, hanging it by a different part each time. Any part that appears to be getting hard should be well rubbed between the hands.

Skins that have been soaked in alum to prevent the hair coming out may have a dirty appearance, and may require cleaning. To do this, well soak them in several changes of warm water, to remove as much of the salt and alum as possible. Now well wash the skins in two or three fresh baths of soap and water. Then rinse in cold water, and finally in water containing a little laundry blue. Then wring out and hang each in the shade to dry. During the drying they should be well worked by pulling, rubbing, shaking, and beating, and the hair brushed.

Before goat skins can be dyed, they must be thoroughly washed in soapsuds, and afterwards in clean water to remove any grease adhering to the hair. For a black dye prepare a mordant bath by dissolving $\frac{3}{4}$ lb. of copperas, 2 oz. of sulphate of copper, and 1 lb. of cream of tartar in 1 gal. of water; heat nearly to boiling, and pass the skin into it; let it stand for one or two hours, then remove and expose to air overnight; then dye in a hot bath made by boiling 5 lb. of logwood chips in 1 gal. of water; remove, wash in cold water, and dry in the open air. For a grey dye soak the skin in a warm bath of $\frac{1}{2}$ lb. of logwood chips in 1 gal. of water; remove, and pass into a mordant bath of 2 oz. of copperas or bichromate of potash in 1 gal. of water. For a brown dye pass the skin into a warm bath of 1 lb. of catechu in 1 gal. of water; allow to remain two hours; remove, and steep in a warm bath of ½ lb. of copper sulphate or sulphate of iron. Experiments should be tried with small pieces of the skins. If the colours are not suitable for the particular skin in hand, alter the proportions of the dye.

In dyeing rabbit skins black, the mordant consists of sulphate of iron (copperas) and acetate of lead (sugar of lead); these two react, the result being a precipitate of sulphate of lead and the formation of acetate of iron. The acetate of iron is really the mordant in this case. In making this solution have it fairly strong—1½ lb. of sulphate of iron and 3 lb. of sugar of lead to 1 gallon. For the dye, quantities of logwood, galls, and turmeric may be varied according to the hue of the black required; try equal parts first—that is, 1 lb. each of logwood chips, galls, and turmeric to 1 gallon, and vary the quantity if the black is not satisfactory. A little sulphate of copper (about 2 oz.) in the mordant is generally an improvement. To keep the backs of the skins free from colour, only brush the liquors on. First apply the mordant, and then the dye; and if the dye does not readily take, again apply the mordant and dye, and so on. Before dyeing, the hair should be carefully washed with soap and water to remove the greasiness; ammonia may be used with advantage when washing.

For dyeing skins, the usual aniline colours do not seem suitable, as after a time they lose their proper tint. But it has been claimed that the colours may be made much faster if they are rubbed with Reimann's composition. This is a solution of 12½ oz. of gum arabic in about 7 pints of water, or of shellac in alcohol in the same quantities. Of course, a smaller quantity may be made, keeping to the proper proportions. The dyed skin is vigorously rubbed with the composition. Reimann also recommends a mixture of $8\frac{1}{2}$ oz. of liquid ammonia and 7 pints of water; this is heated to a temperature of about 167° F., $6\frac{1}{4}$ oz. of caseine is dissolved in it, and the whole stirred till boiling point is reached. When cold, decant, and rub the skin with the clear liquid. Skins so treated may be rendered supple by well rubbing with a mixture of 8 oz. of yolk of egg and 4 oz. of glycerine. Only a little is applied, and when the skin is half dry, it is rubbed with a clean woollen rag until quite dry.

In rendering fox brushes soft and pliable Colonel Park's method of curing skins (see p. 112) can be adopted. But if the brushes have been skinned clean off the tails, not cut down, a somewhat different process must be adopted. The scraping can be done by forming a tool something like the stuffing-iron (Fig. 11, p. 14), but broader. Then the flattened end should be bent at right angles, the edge made sharp and toothed, and the corners removed with a file to prevent cutting the skin. By inserting this into the brushes, the skin can be scraped and the fibres still further loosened by bending and twisting.

To cure a goat's skin, trim it on the flesh side with a sharp knife, and then well brush with a solution of $2\frac{1}{2}$ lb. of alum and 1 lb. of common salt in 1 gal. of warm water; the skin should be treated two or three times with this solution on successive days. Now sprinkle bran all over the skin, brush out, and nail the skin to a board and dry it. As a preservative against insects, the flesh side may be treated with a mixture of arsenic and black pepper previous to drying. All skins have a smell peculiar to themselves, but in most cases these smells are totally removed during the curing and dressing. But if the smell after dressing is very strong, hang the skin frequently in the open air when a fairly strong wind is blowing. If this does not entirely remove the smell, disguise it by adding oil of birch, or sprinkling a few drops of essence of musk on the skin. Both of these are lasting perfumes. The peculiar smell of Russian dressed skins is due to the addition of oil of birch.

For making rugs the treatment of skins with alum and salt, or "tawing," as it is called, is more often resorted to than is the process of tanning. As explained before, the skin is thrown across a bench, and the adhering flesh and fatty tissue either cut or scraped away with a sharp knife. The flesh side of the hide may next be treated for a week or two with a bran mash, which, by a process of fermentation, softens the inner integument, and allows it to be removed. This may prove useful in softening the inner membrane of tough skins, and afterwards allows it to be separated with the knife. The object of this treatment is to remove all material that may afterwards tend to putrefy. Next treat the skin with the preservative mentioned in the previous paragraph, a portion of the solution being made slightly warm, and well rubbed into the skin with a brush. The skin should be allowed to remain damp for a few days, then pinned down tightly stretched on a board, and placed in the sunlight to dry. For tanning skins it matters very little what proportions of material are used. Half fill a copper or earthenware vessel with oak bark chips, and fill up with boiling water; keep simmering for a few hours, then strain. Place the skin in the infusion as soon as it becomes tepid, and allow it to remain for at least three weeks; remove, shake well, peg on a board, and allow to dry. The length of time required in tanning a skin depends upon its thickness and upon the strength of the solution. With a strong solution the time is lessened; but it is not advisable to use a strong infusion at first, or the skin may be only superficially tanned. Treating as above described, three weeks is a fair time to give it.

Hare skins can be cured so as to turn out soft and pliable. The preservative is common table salt 1 lb., and burnt alum 4lb. These are well powdered, mixed, and rubbed into the skin, which is stretched on a flat board as soon as removed from the animal. When dry, it is rubbed down with pumice-stone, or a solution is made of the salt and alum, and the skin is steeped in it, dried, and pumice-stoned, and the process repeated till it is pliable; then it is rubbed with lard, and, when this has had time to soak in and soften, the superfluous grease is removed by thoroughly kneading with plenty of bran. Another way is to nail the freshly stripped skin on a board and cover it with lard. Leave it to soak in for a week, watching it so that any part that threatens to go dry may have more lard applied at once. At the end of the week remove the skin from the board and wash in warm water with soap to remove the surface greasiness. Then let it dry, rolling, rubbing, pulling, and stretching it about in every way possible the while. For freshly stripped cats', rabbits', and similar small skins the following is recommended: Whiting, 2½lb.; soft soap, 1 lb.; chloride of lime, 2 oz; tincture of musk, 1 oz. Boil the soap and whiting together in 1 pint of water, powder the chloride of lime, and then stir it in. When nearly cold, add the musk, stirring it well in. After dressing with this and drying, the larding, washing, and rubbing are proceeded with to finish the skins.

The method described on p. 114 is suitable for a leopard skin. If the skin has been salted, the skin must first be freed from all salt by soaking and steeping it in water, frequently changed. It should then be tawed, that is, made into white leather by steeping and scouring in a bath of bran, alum, and salt, using a gallon of hot water to 1 lb. of alum, ¼ lb. of salt, and, roughly, about ¼ peck of bran. If not already done, all the inside of the skin must be cut and scraped away with a currier's or other sharp knife. It should then be stretched out to its full extent upon a wooden frame and allowed to dry in the shade. When nearly dry, remove the nails, and rub and work the skin with the hands, the action, as before mentioned, being similar to that of washing clothes. The shaving and rubbing must be done perfectly. If necessary, the processes can be repeated. Next, lard is worked into the flesh side of the skin as before described, and then all surface grease is removed with sawdust, with which also the hair is well rubbed; some use bran on the fur side. A vigorous shaking, a few smart strokes with a light cane, followed by a good "grooming" with a scratch-card, will complete the operation. The skin should be as soft as kid, and not affected by climatic variations. The work is extremely dirty and very hard, for the scraping and rubbing must be really thorough. A novice should not make his first attempt on a valuable skin. To mount a leopard skin as a rug, place it upon red cloth and mark with chalk the outline of the skin. Cut this out, and then cut strips of the same material from 4 in. to 6 in. wide. One edge of all these strips is then pinked, scolloped, or pounced to form a border. The skin is now placed upon the cloth shape, the border arranged in pleats or gathers between these, and all stitched together. It would be easier to stitch the border to the skin first, and then sew the cloth shape to the border.

Methods of curing rabbit skins have already been given, but the following gives some more information on the subject. To cure a rabbit skin, it must be fresh flayed and cleaned of all fat and particles of flesh by scraping it with a blunt knife whilst stretched, fur inwards, upon a rounded surface such as a baluster rail. Then steep it in the usual solution of 4 parts alum and 1 part salt. Mix them thoroughly together when dry, and then add as much warm water as will dissolve the mixture. The quantity depends on the size of the skin. To ascertain when it has soaked long enough, squeeze the liquid from it. Then double it, with the skin side outwards, so as to make a crease, and when the line shows white the soaking can be stopped. The soaking usually takes about forty-eight hours. Make a paste of flour and water, and having rinsed the skin dip it for a minute in the warm gruel. Then wash it clean with cold water, and dry it. When about half dry, stretch again on a board, and rub with pumice. Small skins, when freshly flayed, can be cured by being soaked for a few days in a solution of tan. This tan can be made by boiling oak bark or oak galls in rain or distilled water, or by dissolving tannin in soft water. Fill a pot with oak bark, and boil it in twice as much water for three hours. Use the solution cold, and take out and rub the skin as often as possible during the process.

Cats' skins if required to be soft when finished should be tanned. Remove every particle of flesh from the skin, scraping with a blunt knife, but being careful not to injure the skin itself. Dry well by rubbing with towels; and with a scrubbing brush apply to the skin side some hot water and soft soap. Mix together 2 oz. of salts of tartar and 1 oz. of ammonia, both in powder, and sprinkle this on the skin and scrub well to remove the grease. Rub the skin till dry with clean, dry sawdust. Leave for an hour or two, and then pickle it in this mixture: Fine ground oatmeal, 8 oz.; corrosive sublimate (a deadly poison, not to be allowed to touch any scratch or scab on the operator's hands), 4 oz.; saltpetre, 2 oz.; vinegar, 2 qts. Boil the vinegar, and then pour it on the other ingredients, stirring well the while. When quite cold, put the skin in and leave it to soak for forty-eight hours, stirring and working it about as often as possible. Rinse clean, wring it out, and stretch to dry on a board. It will be finished in a week. To soften a stiff skin it has to be rubbed, after tanning, by the hands with an action similar to that used in washing clothes. The use previously of a wooden mallet and a cane switch will reduce the hardness somewhat. Another mixture is alum, 5 lb.; salt, 2 lb.; oatmeal, 2 lb., all finely powdered. Mix with just enough sour milk or buttermilk to make a creamy paste. This is to be rubbed well into the skin side only, whilst the skin is stretched on a firm table. When no more can be worked into the skin, apply a thin surface coating of the mixture, and leave it in a cool place till next day, when add more mixture, working it in with the hands. Repeat this for the third and fourth days, then wash all off, and wring and shake it. When half dry, apply fresh mixture, and go over the five days' operations once more. Then wash thoroughly for some hours in running water till all the mixture is cleaned completely out. Make a saturated solution of alum—that is, dissolve alum in hot water until the water will not dissolve more. Apply this when cool to the skin, and let it dry, stretched on a board in the open air. When dry it will be hard, and must be softened by beating and rubbing. Thorough cleansing with soap and water, and immersion thereafter in water that has had oak bark boiled in it will tan small skins, as is explained in the previous paragraph.

Cured skins, usually more or less hard, can be rendered more pliant by working them with the hands at intervals during the drying, also by stretching and pulling to and fro upon a block of wood; a little curd soap, or yolk of egg, rubbed into the skins while they are wet, will also help to soften them. The smell arising from decomposition may be stopped by adding a little mercuric chloride (corrosive sublimate) to the curing bath, or rubbing in a little white arsenic; both these are deadly poisons. A little oil of citronella or nitrobenzol (oil of mirbane) will disguise the odour.

Sheepskins may be cured by one of the many methods already described. Still another method is to cleanse the wool thoroughly and tack the skin down, fleshy side upwards, on a board. Scrape off all fat and shreds of membrane, then apply plentifully a dressing composed of carbonate of soda 1 part, Hudson's soap, 2 parts, and powdered alum, 3 parts. Let this remain for about a week, occasionally rubbing the powder in and stirring it about, and finally shake off all the surplus powder (which may be preserved for future use), when the skin will be ready for a lining. If for a rug, a pinked border of red baize will set it off to advantage. It may be mounted on the cloth as described on p. 122.

In bleaching a sheepskin the first thing to be done is to clean the wool by using soap and water. Whilst the skin is fresh—that is, newly stripped from the carcase—wash it thoroughly in a solution of soap, made by dissolving one bar in 2 gallons of boiling water, and allowing it to get cool, but not cold, before using. Hot water destroys wool; so does very cold water. Thoroughly pound and wash the wool in 1 qt. of this liquor diluted with 4 qts. of warm water, and with a tablespoonful of paraffin oil in it. Any very dirty patches can be treated first by themselves with a little of the strong liquor. After washing, rinse well in clean, warm water. Dry by squeezing and shaking out.

Do not put the skin in hot sunshine. Dissolve ½ lb. of salt and ½ lb. of alum in 3 pts. of boiling water, and add sufficient cold water to make enough liquor to about cover the skin whilst laid in a shallow tray. Soak it here for twelve hours. Take it out, rinse it well in warm water, and squeeze it dry; passing through a clothes-wringing machine is the best way to dry it. Next rub the skin side with a mixture of half alum, half saltpetre; from 1 oz. to 2 oz. of each is enough for one skin, according to its size. Rub this in for as long as is convenient, or for one or two hours. Fold the skin in two, so as to bring the salted parts together, and put it away for three days, opening it out every day and rubbing it well. At the end of the three days scrape it over with a blunt knife, rub it with pumice-stone, and trim the edges. To actually bleach the wool a further process is necessary. Get a large box without cracks or holes in it, and with one side large enough to allow the skin being spread upon it. Upon this side (inside) tack the skin, so that the flesh side is against the wood and the wool away from it. The skin must be firmly fastened, and must not hang down at the middle or elsewhere. See that the lid fits tight over the top of the box. Put ½ lb. of sulphur in an iron plate, and place this at the bottom of the box. Make a nail red hot, and drop it on the sulphur. Put the lid on, and weight it down. The box should not allow of the fumes escaping; but, as some will find their way out, do the job out of doors. In six or eight hours the fumes of the sulphur will have bleached the wool. When done hang the skin in the open air for the smell to go off. The wool can be combed out with an ordinary comb or a piece of wire carding cloth.

Skins that are very much creased by having been folded can be smoothed by going over the creases with a warm iron having a smooth face; cover as large a space as possible so as not to let the iron stop long enough in one place to damage it.

To remove wool from sheepskins without injuring either the wool or the skins, they are placed in heaps in a warm place until an ammoniacal odour shows that putrefaction has commenced. Then place the skin across an unhairing beam, and with a blunt two-handled dressing-knife remove the hair. By another method, first the wool is sheared off, and then the skins are well soaked in lime-water and placed across a rounded piece of wood or beam; the rest of the hair, wool, etc., together with the greater part of upper scaly skin, is removed by a blunt two-handled knife.

A commercial method of removing wool from sheep skins, as practised at a London fellmonger's yard is the following. First, they are beaten on a wooden block with a mallet to bruise the congealed blood on the necks; then they are thrown into water to rinse the dirt and blood from the wool, and are hung over trestles for the water to drain out. The skins are limewashed on the flesh side, and folded down the back so as to make the bellies match together, being then left for an hour or two so that the lime will set slightly. They are then hung by the thick part of the back of the head upon tenter hooks in large, dark, closed sheds or rooms, and in about two days in the summer the wool will come off quite easily. The sheds have to be heated in the winter. If any grit gets in the lime it will make the "pelt," as it is called, limespecked.

In the North of England the wool is removed in the following manner. The skins are taken either to the riverside or dipped in a water pit to moisten the fleshy side, the wool being kept quite dry. Then they are laid on top of each other, pelt upwards, and lime, of the thickness of batter, is applied with a mop. The skins are taken off and laid flat on the ground, pelt to pelt, in heaps of eight or ten. They remain two days in this condition, and are next taken to the riverside or other convenient place and thoroughly washed to remove all lime and dirt. Next, they are doubled so that the bellies match each other, and are put on a wooden horse to dry over night. While still doubled they are hung up on rails to dry. In winter they are put into a heated room for the same purpose. When dry, they are taken into the "pulling shop," where each man takes one on his "beam" and draws the wool off with his hands, sorting it into four or five qualities. The pelts are put into lime water to remain till sold to the tanner. Skins that have been shorn—known as shearlings—are put into a large shallow pit when they have been "limed" for two or three days, and covered with water. Then follow the various processes of long-wooled skins till they are ready for removing the wool from the pelt. This is done by means of a blunt knife, with two handles at each end, called a rubbing knife.

Sheep skins often are dyed, but before they will take any dye they must be soaked in a solution of carbonate of ammonia and well washed in a solution of soft soap and soda (say 1 lb. of soda to 1 gal. of water) to free them from dirt and grease. They are now ready for dyeing. Aniline dyes are cheapest, but by themselves are fugitive, and therefore require something to fix them (see p. 118). Acetic acid will do this for the greens and blues, and so will vinegar. In the case of reds, prepare a boiling solution of sumach 1 part, alum 5 parts, tartar 2½ parts, and in this place the wool. Then place it in the dye. Sulphate of indigo (1 lb. to 1 gal. of water) may be used for blue; if not dark enough, increase the indigo to 2 lb.

Tropæolin orange with a small quantity of acid

brown will yield a golden brown, the intensity of which may be varied by altering the proportions of the two dyes. A bronze green may be obtained by a mixture of fast green and acid brown. Alkali blue may be used for blues, methyl violet for violets, picric acid for pale yellow, magenta for the colour of that name, eosin for pink, rose, etc. For a black, boil ¾ lb. of copperas, 2 oz. of sulphate of copper, and 1 lb. of cream of tartar in 1 gal. of water. This is the fixing bath. The dye is made by boiling 5 lb. of logwood in 1 gal. of water. For a grey dye, boil ½ lb. of logwood in 1 gal. of water; for the fixing bath, boil 2 oz. of copperas in 1 gal. of water. To make a brown dye, boil 1 lb. of catechu in 1 gal. of water; and for the fixing bath boil ½ lb. of sulphate of copper in 1 gal. of water. These proportions may be varied according to the tint desired. After the skins are dressed and softened, they should be placed in the dye (temperature from 120 to 140 degrees F.), wool downwards, and allowed to remain for an hour or two. They should then be washed in cold water, and hung up to dry till the next day. Then they should be put into the hot fixing solution, allowed to remain for an hour or two, washed in cold water, and hung up to dry. As it is only necessary to immerse the wool in the solutions, some strips of wood can be placed along the bath containing the dye to prevent the skin sinking. Take great care that the solutions are hot when used, and, during the drying, frequently shake the skins and rub them to prevent them drying hard. Repeat the operations if the colour is not intense enough. Try the colour on a waste piece of skin first.

Sheepskin mats or rugs that are hard, and crackle when walked over, can be softened first by reducing their thickness and then by applying grease. The skin, if very thick, should be reduced by scraping with a rounded rasp or curry-comb whilst nailed out flat on a firm, hard table. When all inequalities have been levelled, rub, with considerable force, a little fresh lard or vaseline over every part till the skin has become soft and pliant. The process may be resumed time after time for several days. When thoroughly soft, the skin should be well rubbed for several days with sawdust that does not contain resin, or with bran, to get off all the greasiness that rises to the surface. Finally, some pipeclay should be rubbed vigorously into the restretched skin, and left to see if it discolours with the grease. Beat and scrape off any discoloured pipeclay, and put a new lot on till it remains for twenty-four hours without exhibiting signs of greasiness. Then brush and clean the hair side, using a large, clean cotton cloth dipped in paraffin and wrung out dry. Rub the hair hard; then rinse the dirt out in the paraffin, and repeat the process till all dirt is removed. The sheepskin can be cleaned with soap and water, as described on pp. 115 and 116.

Snake skins can be softened by soaking in water for a night; they should then be soft enough to unroll. Soaking should be carried far enough to enable the skins to be opened without force, but must not be prolonged. By using warm water, about an hour's soaking may suffice.

In curing and dressing an otter's skin, as the long hairs have their roots in the deeper parts of the skin, it is the usual plan among furriers to dress the skin, and then thin and curry it, during which the longer roots of the coarse hair will be cut through, and a smart brushing will remove most of the loosely-held hairs. Any remaining must be pulled away by hand. There is no alternative, as if the thickness of the skin be reduced sufficiently to cut through the shorter hair roots there is danger of spoiling the skin.

Strips of rhinoceros hide sometimes are cured, and walking-sticks made from the strips; first they must be straightened by damping and suspending from a nail with a weight at the lower end, and when thoroughly dry they should be trimmed by knife, rasp, file, emery, etc., and made as smooth as possible. Now French polish them without any "stopping," thus allowing the polish to penetrate. When a good surface has been obtained and a ferrule put on, the work is complete. This produces a semi-transparent appearance, tinted by the polish, and broken abruptly by large dark, or even black, patches. The usual preservatives replace the semi-transparent appearance by a whitish opaque appearance, similar to wood, and cause the elasticity to suffer.

CHAPTER VII.

PRESERVING INSECTS AND BIRDS' EGGS.

COLLECTORS of butterflies and moths generally place the freshly caught insects in envelopes and "set" them at home. The usual method of killing an insect is to pinch it under the wings between the finger and thumb, its wings being kept close together, thus preventing the "view side" from being rubbed. A small square of paper is now creased as shown by the dotted lines in Fig. 81. By folding 1 over 2 and 3 over 1 a triangular envelope is formed, into which the insect is dropped; fold 4 over 3, and the insect will be in the position shown by Fig. 82. Instead of pinching the insects, they may be killed in a "killing bottle," made by pouring into a 4-oz. wide-mouthed stoppered jar 1 oz. of cyanide of potassium, and covering it with wet plaster-of-paris. Shake the bottle as the plaster is setting, so that it forms an even surface, and, when quite set, cover the plaster with a piece of blotting-paper to absorb the moisture and to keep the insect from contact with the damp plaster. This blotting-paper should be renewed when necessary. The cyanide is a deadly poison, so must be used with care, and the bottle kept corked. Put the insect into the bottle, cork it up, and leave the insect in for about ten or fifteen minutes. A few drops of strong spirits of ammonia poured on a piece of cotton-wool in a bottle will also form a killing bottle. Bruised laurel leaves may also be put into a bottle, and prussic acid will be given off, thus forming another killing bottle. A few drops of chloroform poured upon blotting-paper at the bottom of a bottle will also stupefy the insects to death. As soon as an insect is quite dead, remove it from the bottle, catching hold of it by the middle—that is, where the legs join the body—and use a pair of tweezers, not fingers or anything as clumsy. Suitable tweezers can be bought at many shops, and can be made by bending double a strip of thin sheet steel or brass ⅜ in. or ½ in. wide and 6 in. or 8 in. long till the two ends meet and form a delicate substitute for forefinger and thumb. The spring of the metal at the bend should keep the ends

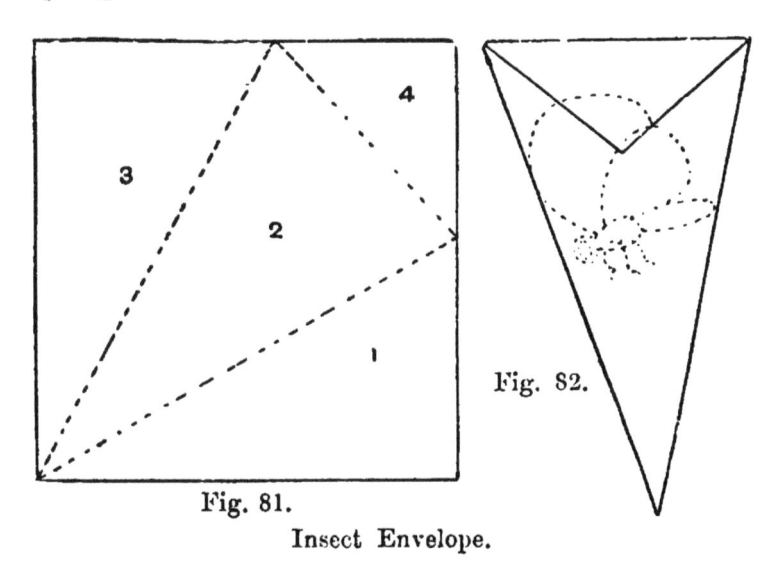

Fig. 81.
Fig. 82.
Insect Envelope.

about ¾ in. or 1 in. apart. The ends can be filed to a blunt point. Touch the insect as little as possible, and always catch hold of it by the thorax. The wings and other parts are covered with minute scales, which are ruffled, rubbed off, and defaced at the slightest touch. The dead insect stiffens and dries up rapidly; therefore, have ready a setting board, on which to hold it in position whilst drying. A common system is to leave the killed insects to dry unset, so that they may be relaxed and set properly at leisure. Dry insects are easily relaxed, and then they may be treated on the setting board precisely as if they had but just been killed.

To relax insects, a simple but risky method is to put them on a piece of cardboard and place this on the bricks of a damp cellar, covering the card, of course, to exclude all dust and rubbish. By this means it is quite possible to get out the wings gradually when the specimen is of fair size. A better method is to put them into a tin box in which is placed a rather shallow bed of damp sand. At the end of a day or so it will be an easy matter to transfer them to a proper setting board and strap down the wings by means of paper braces secured by pins. The sand in the relaxing box should not be too damp, or the specimens will be ruined. Special relaxing boxes are sold by dealers in entomological materials.

A setting board for insects is made by glueing two strips of soft, smooth cork, each 9 in. by 1 in. by $\frac{3}{16}$ in., to a piece of grooved wood 9 in. by 2¼ in. by ½ in. or so. The two cork strips are glued to the wood with a ¼-in. groove between their longer edges, and the cork is slightly bevelled off on the outer edge (see Fig. 83). Insect setting boards used by Continental naturalists are, however, quite flat; but English naturalists consider insects to be spoilt if set flat. Of course, the larger the insect the wider will the board require to be. In the ¼-in. groove the body of the insect lies whilst its wings are extended over the cork on each side. Along the bottom of the central groove glue a strip of cork. Having laid the dead insect in the groove, a pin is pushed vertically through the centre of its thorax down into the cork; the height of the latter should be just sufficient to bring the wing above the edge of the side cork, and packing must be inserted where necessary to ensure this.

Braces for securing the wings of insects on setting boards are of thin card cut into strips about 1½ in.

long, or longer if the insects are large — ⅛ in. is the width of the widest end. The actual process of setting a butterfly or moth is as follows. Taking up an insect, pass a suitably sized entomological pin through the centre of the thorax, being careful not to push off the legs. Now select a setting board (shown in section by Fig. 83) with a groove A wide enough for the body, and with sides broad enough

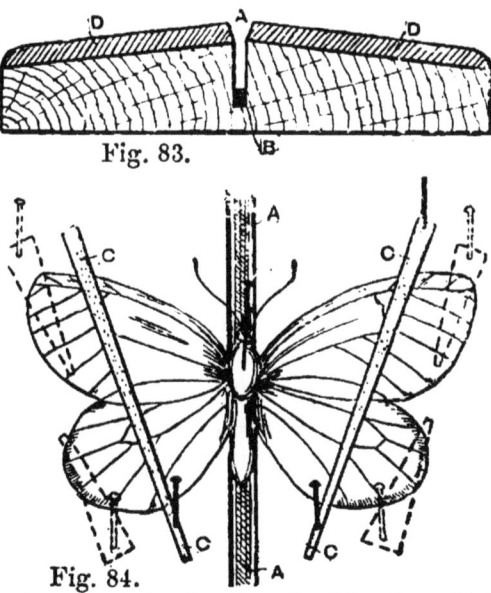

Fig. 83.

Fig. 84.

Fig. 83.—Section of Setting Board. Fig. 84.—Butterfly on Setting Board.

to support the wings, and, placing the body in the groove, press the pin into the cork B at the bottom of the groove. The wings are now standing upright and close together. Take one of the card strips or braces C (see Fig. 84), place it between the wings, and gently draw one wing towards the setting board. Having brought this wing nearly down, with ordinary pins pushed through the ends of the brace, fasten the wing in this position to the cork of the setting board, D, Fig. 83.

The " pin " which passes through the thorax may be a long, thin needle fixed in a light cane handle, say 1 in. long, or preferably an entomological pin, long and thin with a small head, such as are sold specially for the purpose. If the wings can be spread with a couple of sparrow-tail or flight feathers fixed in a handle, all the better. Contact with fingers or tweezers or such like spoils the wings. Now, with a fine needle, working from the underside of the wing, gently move the upper wing towards the body. Having spread these satisfactorily, press the pins in the brace firmly into the cork D, so that the wing is brought into contact with the setting board. Treat the other wing in the same way, and see that the wings form corresponding angles on both sides. One, or perhaps two braces for each wing will be quite sufficient. The antennæ may be bent down and fixed by pins alone. These are very brittle, and, if broken off, should be fixed with cement. Fig. 84 shows the method of bracing the butterflies. The dotted lines are smaller braces, which may either supplement the larger ones or replace them. Put the set insect aside for a week or so, remove the straps, and pin the specimen inside a store box or case.

Caterpillars may be preserved in the following way. Press out the contents of the body with the fingers, working from the head to the tail, and dragging away the mass with a crochet needle. Great care must be exercised. Now place the end of a fine blowpipe in the orifice at the tail end and blow up the empty skin and keep it distended till dry. This drying must be hastened by artificial means. Some use a glass jar over a spirit lamp in which to place the skin while blowing; but an ordinary "box-iron" may be used, heated in the same manner as in the laundry. Heat an iron, place it in the box, close the slide, and leave it till the box is hot. Then take out the iron, place the skin in, and blow it up. In a short time it will be dry, but, of course, the air must not be allowed to escape until the skin is dry. Do not unnaturally distend the skin, and do not allow the skin to touch any part of the heated box, or it will be burnt and, of course, spoilt.

As regards beetles, it is advisable, unless there are good reasons for delay, to kill the beetles as soon as caught, as some specimens are likely to be damaged by long captivity. If, however, they must be kept alive till home is reached, each specimen must be kept alone. If kept together in one receptacle, they not only damage each other in their efforts to escape, but the carnivorous kinds devour the others. To set a beetle, pin it through the right elytron (wing case) with an entomological pin, raising the body high enough to give sufficient space for the proper arrangement of the legs. The beetle is then pinned to a flat piece of cork, and the legs arranged, each joint of the legs being kept in position with common pins. Pins are also used to display the antennæ, and the specimen is then left for a few days to dry. When dry, the common pins are withdrawn, and the beetle is removed to the specimen drawer and pinned down on a card bearing its common and its scientific name. Beetles may also be set with gum. On a piece of card drop a little gum where the legs of the beetle are likely to come. Pin the beetle upon the card, and draw each leg into position and keep it there till the gum has set. Then put the specimen away to dry, and when set release from the card by dipping into warm water; then lightly touch the underside of the feet with gum, and place upon a clean card, bearing name, date, locality, etc. The beetles may also be set by means of card braces or pins, left to dry, and placed in the cabinet with the name, etc., upon a separate card. The first method of setting beetles described above is the one to be preferred.

The setting of insects having been dealt with in sufficient detail, information on preserving eggshells may be given.

In order to blow eggs without making more than one hole, two tools are necessary—a drill and a blowpipe, which may be either purchased or made. The egg drills sold by naturalists have the ends formed much like the rose of a woodworker's countersink, and cost from 1d. to 6d., but a substitute may quickly be formed by filing the end of a piece of steel wire into a square point. Round wire will answer if the edges of the point are left sharp, but the best wire is the pinion wire used by watchmakers. This should be filed to a point, then the channels should be relieved by a triangular file.

The other tool is a blowpipe, which may be made from a piece of glass tubing, obtainable from the chemist. One end should be heated and drawn to a point. These blowpipes may be bought ready made for about 2d., or much better and finer ones, made of metal, for 6d. To use them, the egg should be held by the left fingers, and the drill by the right hand. Then, placing the drill on the egg, exactly in the centre of the side, and rotating by a kind of circular motion between the finger and the thumb, a perfectly round hole is made.

To blow an egg, place the finer end of the blowpipe *near* the hole (some say in the hole) and blow. The contents of the egg will be quickly forced out by the air. When all is clear, rinse out the shell with water containing a few drops of oil of cloves, to prevent putrefaction. Now place the shell, hole downwards, upon a piece of blotting paper, which will readily absorb any moisture left inside. When dry, cover the hole with a small piece of gummed paper to exclude dust, and the eggshell is ready for the collection.

To prevent birds' eggs cracking or crumbling after they are blown, well rinse them out with corrosive sublimate dissolved in spirits of wine (a few grains to the ounce); this is a deadly poison. Insert a small quantity into the egg by means of a glass egg-blower with a bulb, then shake the egg so that the solution comes out of the egg by the blower, and return it to the bottle. Now place the egg with the hole resting upon blotting-paper, so that the last drop or two may be drawn out, and finally cover the hole with a small piece of gummed paper. Water containing a few drops of oil of cloves may be used in place of the sublimate if desired.

Cabinets in which insects and eggs are kept are of many different kinds. The first arrangement to

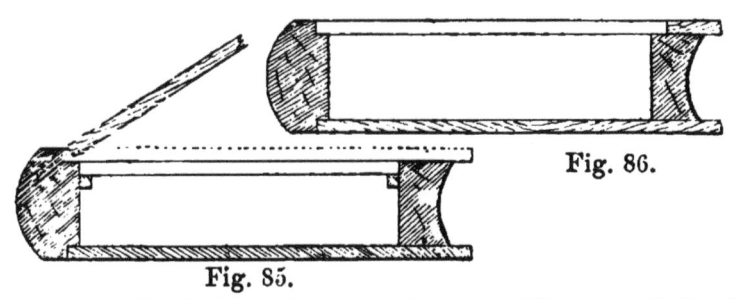

Fig. 86.

Fig. 85.

Fig. 85.—Single Book Box for Insects. Fig. 86.—Half of Double Book Box for Insects.

be mentioned is an exhibition case in the form of a book, of which a section is shown by Fig. 85. One cover, the lower one, is a fixture, but the other is hinged to the back. The glass under this latter cover rests upon small slips of wood glued inside the case, and is finally fixed, when the specimens are complete and the case is filled, by pasted slips of ornamental paper. Some of these box cases have the back of (say) mahogany with the bands of another wood, either ebony or whitewood, but it is far better to cover the back with leather, fix upon this the title in gilt, and well tool the back; the result will be to all intents and purposes a volume. Bookbinders usually fix the leather upon the backs of books by means of good flour paste, but cloth requires glue. It is not usual, however, to see these single book-boxes; generally two are hinged together at the back, opening therefore in front. In this case the section would be as in Fig. 86. Of course, when the volumes are not open the glass cover of the one faces (and would touch but for the paper binding) the glass cover of the other, thus keeping all the interior dark, a necessary con-

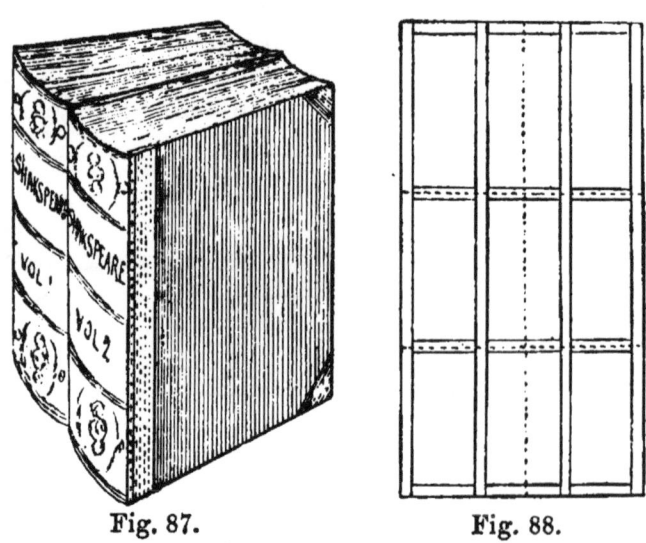

Fig. 87.   Fig. 88.

Fig. 87.—Double Book Box for Insects. Fig. 88.—Cork Lining of Insect Cabinet.

dition with entomological specimens, as light, and especially sunshine, really causes the colours of many butterflies and moths to fade. Fig. 87 shows the appearance of the hinged book-box when finished.

The bottom requires to be covered with cork in order to support the pins. The cork used is cut specially for this purpose, and is known as "cabinet" or "entomological" cork; it is sold in sheets of three or four principal sizes, but being only about $\frac{1}{8}$ in.

or $\frac{3}{16}$ in. thick it does not give too much hold to the pins. Therefore some cut a few sheets of cork into $\frac{1}{4}$-in. strips, and glue these upon the part to be corked, and then fasten the sheets upon these with glue. (See Fig. 88, in which the bars or strips are shown by continuous lines and the sheets by dotted lines.) The pins can now be thrust to twice the depth.

The upper surface of the cork should be well dressed with emery cloth or sandpaper to smooth and level joinings, and should then be covered with white blotting-paper. It will be advisable to put a few drops of carbolic acid in all the pastes, etc., used in this work. Also sprinkle some car-

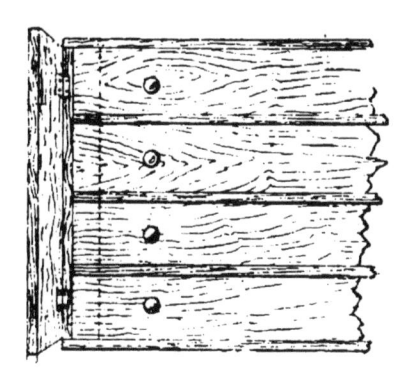

Fig. 89.—Drawers with Hinged Pillar.

bolic powder or insect powder in the spaces between the strips of cork before placing the sheets of cork in position. Some also recommend that the cork be soaked in a solution of corrosive sublimate, in order to minimise the evil effects so frequently wrought by the destructive "mites." Camphor is popularly thought to keep away these mites, and a small quantity of this is usually placed in each box or drawer. A small triangular space may be formed for this purpose at one or more corners by means of a bit of wood, or even card.

Cabinets proper are really nothing more than chests of drawers, but these have to be constructed so skilfully that practical cabinet makers find it no easy work. Cabinets may be made of many woods and of various sizes. The best woods are Spanish mahogany, oak, and deal. Cedar had better be avoided owing to its peculiar property of giving out a gummy substance, which may possibly settle upon the wings of the insects or upon the birds' eggs and thus spoil them. It is very essential, too, that whatever wood is used it should be well seasoned, because the slightest crevice will allow dust and insects to get in, and perhaps nullify a collection of insects and eggs the trophy of years of patient work.

It may be advisable to give a list of the kind of cabinets generally seen:—1. Plain deal, stained and polished to imitate mahogany or walnut. Deal ebonised and polished, then relieved in parts with gold, is not so often seen, but is very effective. 2. Polished deal, with drawer fronts veneered. 3. Polished deal drawer fronts, with veneered glass panel doors. 4. Polished deal, with mahogany glass panel doors. 5. Polished deal, with mahogany rolled pillars. 6. Plain mahogany, polished. 7. Polished mahogany, with glass panel door. 8. Polished mahogany, with rolled pillars. For many reasons the drawers should be so arranged as to be kept closed when desired, and for this reason the cabinet should be provided with glazed doors or with two pillars hinged to the upright edges of the carcase, so that each covers about an inch of the end of the drawers. Fig. 89, p. 141, shows one of these pillars open, and the dotted line shows the part covered when closed. A lock upon one of these pillars makes it impossible to open the drawers; thus, only one of the hinged pillars need be provided with lock, etc., as the second pillar is introduced mainly for the sake of symmetry.

The following is a list of standard sizes of entomological cabinets:—

Number of Drawers.	Height.	Width.	Depth.
4	12 in.	13 in.	8 in.
6	16½ in.	15 in.	9 in.
8	22 in.	18 in.	11 in.
10	27½ in.	19½ in.	12 in.
12	33½ in.	19½ in.	16½ in.
14	38½ in.	19½ in.	16½ in.
16	43½ in.	19½ in.	16½ in.
18	48 in.	19½ in.	16½ in.
20	53 in.	19½ in.	16½ in.

In the five latter, the size of the drawers is usually 17 in. by 15 in., running on rails.

Cabinets for birds' eggs are not corked, but instead each drawer is divided by partitions into a number of compartments, varying in size according to the eggs intended to occupy these divisions. The usual dimensions, in inches, are:—

Drawers.	Divisions.	Height.	Width.	Depth.
4	75	13 in.	12 in.	9½ in.
6	122	18½ in.	15 in.	9½ in.
8	238	25 in.	19 in.	11 in.
10	348	33 in.	22 in.	14 in.
11	371	38 in.	26 in.	18 in.

Eggs may be arranged very well in shallow wooden trays.

Spread some white or pink wadding or cotton-wool upon each tray, and then make a depression in the centre, and in this place the egg, hole downwards. To arrange them, divide them into the following classes:—1. Raptores or prey catchers (hawks and owls). 2. Insessores or perchers (most birds). 3. Rasores or scratchers (doves, game, ostrich). 4. Grallatores or waders (shore birds, herons, woodcocks, rails, coots, etc.). 5. Natadores or swimmers (ducks and gulls).

Having selected the wood and decided upon the size and number of drawers, the cabinet may be made. The work of constructing an egg cabinet consists of three independent parts: (1) making the carcase or frame of the whole, (2) making the drawers, and (3) covering the drawers with glass.

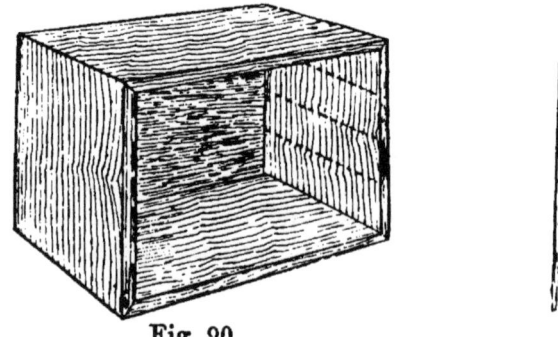

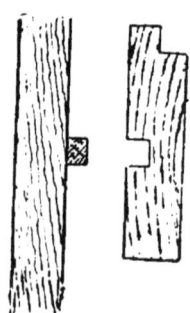

Fig. 90. Fig. 91.

Fig. 90.—Body of Cabinet. Fig. 91.—Drawer Section showing Groove and Runner.

The carcase may be made exactly like an ordinary chest of drawers, and Fig. 89 gives a sketch of a part of a cabinet of this form.

The next form of egg cabinet has outside walls only, as shown in Fig. 90. Here the drawers touch their neighbours, at least in front, and are not separated as in Fig. 89, p. 141. Therefore some arrangement must be made for sliding the drawers in. This must take the form of either a groove cut in the side of the drawer in which slides a runner attached to the inner side of the carcase, or *vice versâ*. The dotted lines in Fig. 90 show the position of these grooves. Fig. 91 shows the section of part of a

EGG AND INSECT CABINETS. 145

drawer provided with a groove ploughed out to receive a runner fastened to the inside of the framework or carcase. This is the best arrangement, and the exercise of a little ingenuity will enable it to be so made as not to disfigure the front. Fig. 92 shows a simple method of accomplishing this. It consists in simply halving the end of the front piece, and not allowing the groove to be cut through the front part which is left.

Fig. 93 gives a similar section to Fig. 91, but with the runner and the groove reversed. This is

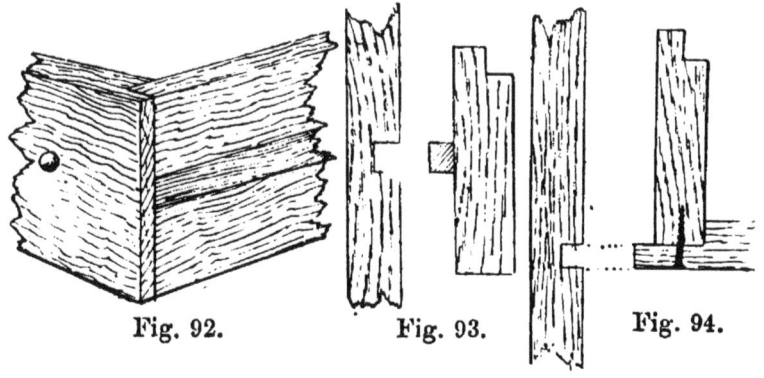

Fig. 92.   Fig. 93.   Fig. 94.

Fig. 92.—Drawer with Grooved Side. Figs. 93 and 94.—Drawer Sections showing Grooves and Runner.

not nearly so good as the method shown by Fig. 91, as the front is necessarily disfigured by the runner showing. Sometimes the drawers are arranged as in Fig. 94, in which the runner is formed by the bottom of the drawer being prolonged sufficiently to go into the channel. But, for both ease in construction and neatness in appearance, preference must certainly be given to the method shown by Fig. 91.

It is an advantage to have the cabinet drawers so arranged that they cannot be drawn quite out, thus obviating the risk of the drawer coming out upon the floor with a crash, ruining probably both

J

the drawer and its contents. This may easily be arranged by placing a screw through the side of the frame and near the front, the point of which should work in the groove cut deeply enough for the runner, but not for the screw, consequently the drawer is stopped upon the back reaching the screw.

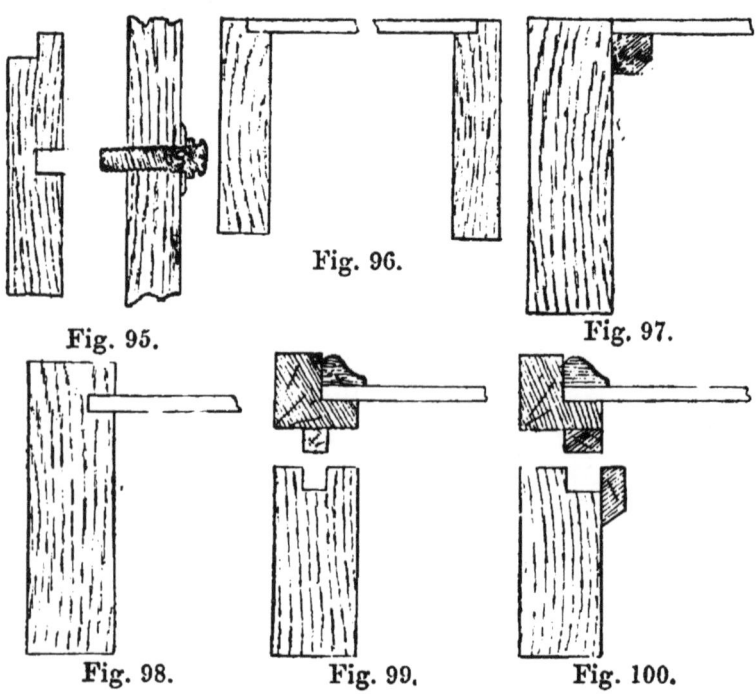

Fig. 95.—Screw to Prevent Drawers Coming Out. Figs. 96 to 100.—Fixing Glass in Drawers.

Fig. 95 shows a brass screw arranged for this purpose, but an ordinary wood screw will answer equally well, although it is not quite so easily taken out should the drawer require removal. A screw at one end only will answer as well as one at both ends of the cabinet. It is in the part of the work just described that the difficulty of making a really first-class cabinet comes in. The drawers ought to be perfectly interchangeable, and this should apply whether the drawers fit into the carcase by runners or by the tongues and grooves just described.

The method of fixing the glass cover upon each drawer needs explanation. Several methods of doing this are shown in Figs. 96 to 101. (1) The first method, illustrated by Fig. 96, simply consists of the glass dropping into a space formed by rebating out a space from the inner surface of the drawer itself or by fixing inside the drawer four strips of wood to support the glass, as in Fig.

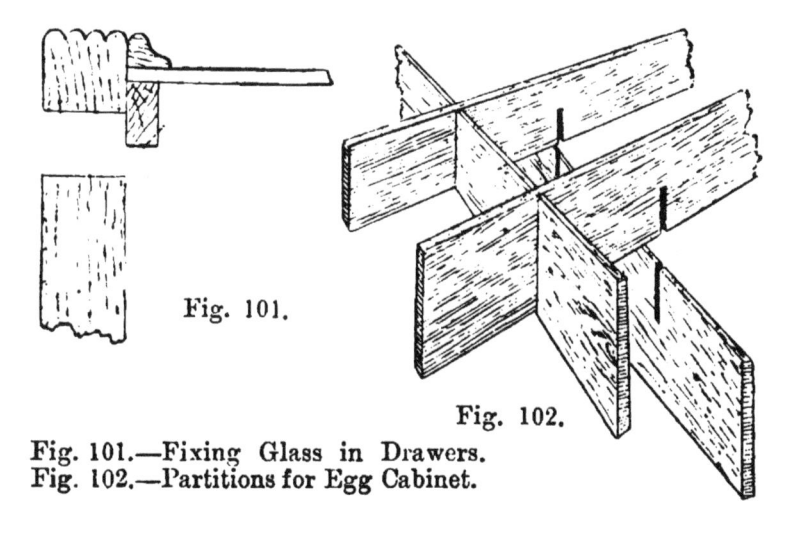

Fig. 101.

Fig. 102.

Fig. 101.—Fixing Glass in Drawers.
Fig. 102.—Partitions for Egg Cabinet.

97. Fig. 96 is the better as regards neatness, but neither is recommended, as dust, etc., can readily get between the glass and wood. Velvet glued along the rebate will somewhat obviate this, but the only case in which this method should be used is when the drawer is complete and there is no likelihood of its contents being disturbed. Then the glass may be fixed down by means of pasted strips of paper, and the case thus made air-tight as well as dust-tight. (2) Fig. 98 shows another method sometimes used. A groove is ploughed out along the inside of each side and the front, into

which the glass slides from the back, which is lowered for this purpose. (3) A better plan, but a more difficult one to carry out, is to set the glass into a frame which will exactly cover the top of the drawer, and in the bottom of this frame to form a tongue fitting into a groove in the top of the drawer. The top of the drawer may in this case be covered with velvet, and then no dust can possibly enter. (See Figs. 99 and 100.) (4) Another method is a modification of No. 1. In this the glass is framed, and this frame is hinged to the top of the drawer and drops into the rebate formed in the four walls of the drawer. (5) In another form (Fig. 101) the frame into which the glass is fixed exactly corresponds in size with that of the drawer upon which it drops. Dust is excluded by a fillet or tongue fixed to the inner surface of the frame, and just large enough to fit into the drawer. (6) In other cases the glass is puttied in on the top, and thus is a fixture. The bottom is fixed by screws, which must be removed to allow of any change being made inside.

The drawers of egg cabinets need not be corked; they are best divided into compartments by thin ($\frac{1}{8}$-in.) wood, as shown by Fig. 102. Each compartment then is lined with cotton-wool. Sometimes the drawers are plain, the fixed partitions being replaced by cardboard boxes lined with wadding, but this is not a plan often adopted. If it is desirable to keep the nests, each should be placed in a separate cardboard box provided with a glazed top. These can then be placed side by side in a drawer deep enough to contain them.

CHAPTER VIII.

CASES FOR STUFFED SPECIMENS.

THE making of cases for stuffed specimens will be dealt with in this, the concluding, chapter. The commonest, and at the same time the most useful, case is the ordinary box case, with glass in front only, which is made thus. Each piece of wood is first dressed and squared; then, with a fillister, about half the depth is cut out along each edge. To fit the case together, it is first glued and then nailed from both end and side. This makes it thoroughly dust-proof and firm. Fig. 103 shows the joint. The rebate at the back receives the wooden back, which is fixed there with glue and brads. The front rebate is for the glass, held in place by a fine mitred beading; or it may be fixed by strips of paper pasted to both wood and glass, or both paper and beading may be used at the same time. Gilt moulding may be used outside the glass instead of the beading, or, as is preferable, inside the glass, in addition to beading.

In the glass-ended case, the front and two ends are of glass, and the top, bottom, and back of wood, rebated and fixed as described above. To prevent the back joints giving way, uprights are fixed between the top and bottom at the front corners. In small cases these uprights may be of wire bolted into both top and bottom, and will be afterwards hidden by the paper binding. In larger cases, the uprights should be of wood; in plain cases only a $\frac{1}{4}$ in. strip, with the inside corner rounded off, serves as an upright. These also will be hidden by narrow strips of black paper, which are pasted down the vertical edges of the glass to hide their junction. Better cases have the uprights ¾ in. square, with rebates for the glass cut on opposite sides (Fig. 104). The outer corner should be nicely rounded off. This case may carry a piece of moulding both on the top and bottom.

An easily made fancy case may have bamboo uprights fixed on the outside of the glass (see Fig. 105). Thin strips of bamboo can replace the beading at the top and bottom of the glass, while moulding, etc., can be formed of bamboo split down the middle and glued and pinned to wood. The

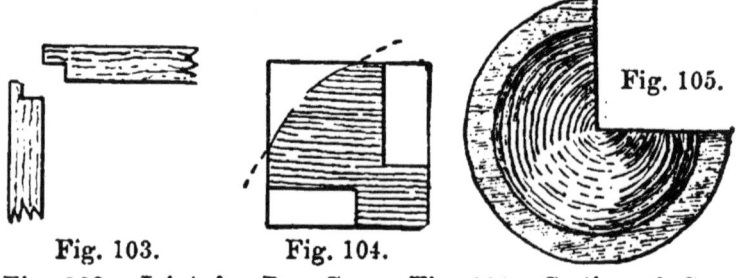

Fig. 103. Fig. 104. Fig. 105.

Fig. 103.—Joint for Box Case. Fig. 104.—Section of Case Upright. Fig. 105.—Section of Bamboo Cane Upright.

working of bamboo is dealt with fully in the companion handbook, "Bamboo Work."

The canted cornered case is mentioned solely that it may be condemned. A plan of it is given in Fig. 106, A B and C D being the sides and B C the back, all of wood. The remaining part, A E F D, is glass. It need scarcely be said that at E and F will be two black lines, which will either make the triangular parts B A E and C D F quite useless, or spoil the appearance of anything put into them.

The best cases for fish are those in which the glass is curved. Fig. 107 is the plan of a case for swimming fish; A B, C D, and B C are the wood sides and back, and A D the curved glass front. Fig. 108 is a section through a case suitable for fish lying upon a bank: A B is the back, B C the bottom, both of wood, and A C is the bent glass. Sometimes birds are put into these cases.

Glass shades are of three kinds—the undesirable round shape; oval, which are rather better; and square, which are the best and most expensive. Far neater and better in every way are "mounts," which are simply the tops of round shades fitting into turned stands. These are very neat, and with one or two little birds (say goldfinches), and some nice grasses, form really handsome ornaments to hang upon a wall. The glass is fixed in the stand

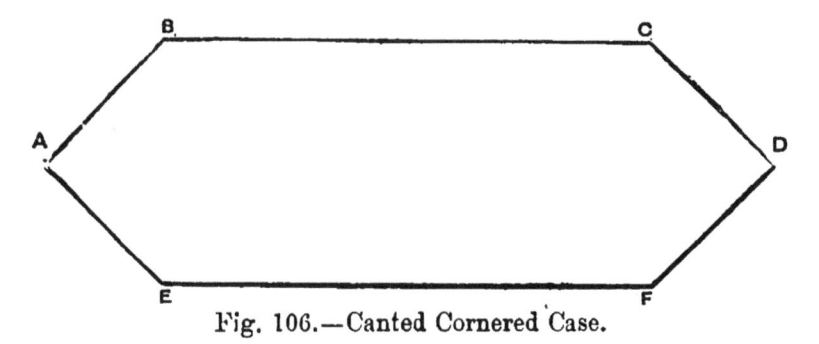

Fig. 106.—Canted Cornered Case.

with plaster-of-paris mixed with water. The junction may be hidden by a band of colour or gilt, but the usual method is by a band of chenille. One kind of mount may be made of five pieces of glass, with a bottom of wood, this having a rebate along each edge and the glasses being fastened together by strips of paper or tape. Large cases may be made in this way, and bamboo strips put along each edge outside, cut from the bamboo canes as in Fig. 105.

The case is ebonised as follows. Into some hot, thin glue, stir enough lampblack to form a paint and brush this well into the case, etc., while still hot. When dry, smooth it, if required, with emery paper, and then coat with brunswick black or japan black. With regard to the finishing of the inside, the back may be ploughed out deeply enough to take in a piece of canvas stretched upon a wooden frame. Upon this some appropriate scene is painted in oil colours. In this case, probably the top and ends would also be covered with canvas and coloured, and the glass might be fixed with putty. This is the only case in which the glass may be thus fixed, for if the lining is of paper the oil in the putty will spread all over it, completely spoiling it. In most cases the inside is covered with paper, pasted on, and then coloured with distemper, and the colours used for this purpose are dry white lead, lime blue, carmine, and chrome

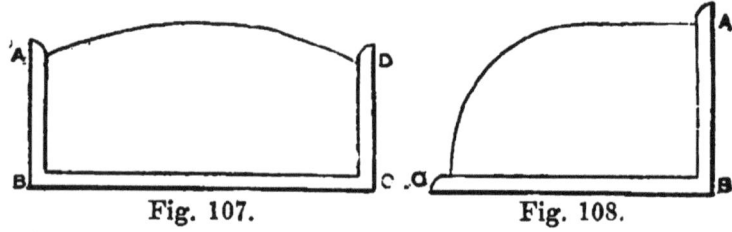

Fig. 107.   Fig. 108.

Figs. 107 and 108.—Sections of Fish Cases having Bent Glass Fronts.

yellow; the white lead, it is thought, is less liable to be streaky than whiting. A small quantity of blue should be mixed with the white for a toned sky, and half way down the back the yellow may be introduced, gradually increasing in colour till the bottom part is a bright yellow. If some light streaks of carmine are introduced, a good idea of sunset, with floating fleecy clouds, will be produced. But very little of the carmine must be used.

The paper for the insides of the cases may be good cartridge paper, but what is known by paperhangers as white linings or ceiling paper is also very suitable. The paper used for fixing the glass and for covering the upright edges in the smaller cases is black glazed foolscap. Scenes may be painted in distemper upon the inside instead of putting in a toned sky only; and one or two large grasses or flowers are finally painted across the whole.

Having the case made, coloured, and papered, the purpose in view will be served by describing how to place, say, a stuffed bird inside it; the bird will have been stuffed as described in Chapter II., and must be thoroughly dry. The points noted on pp. 36 to 39 should be studied. As the object is to represent the bird in the midst of its natural surroundings, the soil or rock must be replaced by something light, and yet so like the original substance that the difference is not noticeable. Brown paper is the material used for this purpose. It is a good plan, in all cases, to make a false bottom, fix the rockwork, etc., upon this; then put in the whole, fastening it with fine screws from the bottom.

Having cut the piece or pieces of, say, $\frac{1}{4}$ in. stuff (old boxes will do) as large as the bottom of the case, chamfer the ends and front (if a glass-ended case is used), then fix the bird, or birds, by means of strips of wood in the position and at the height thought most suitable. Suppose that at one end a hillock is wanted; get a piece of straight brown paper, fasten one edge down with gimp pins, push some shavings or paper under it, dust some carbolic powder or insect powder among it, and draw down the other end towards the false bottom, fastening this again with gimp pins. After having made the other edges safe, proceed to form other hillocks where it is thought they are required. Continue this until there is some rough likeness to the sketch that should always be made before beginning this work. Now get some finer paper; the best to use is the thin, light brown, wrapping paper used by drapers. Tearing off a little piece, perhaps as big as a penny, cover this with paste, and proceed to join the hillocks together. This is a tiresome job, but everything now depends upon the thoroughness with which this is done. All creases and sharp edges must be hidden, all the hillocks joined together (in the valleys), and the edges of the brown paper well pasted down to the bottom with it. Use only small pieces of paper, and plenty of paste.

Leave the work until it is dry, and then mix enough plaster-of-paris with some hot, thin glue to make a cream. Then with a small brush cover every part of the groundwork with this composition while it is still hot, putting it on with no sparing hand. Probably by the next day it will be dry. Then paint it with thin glue and dash on plenty of sharp sand (silver sand is the best). The whole of the glue must be hidden by the sand, and therefore this must be thrown on rather forcibly.

When dry, proceed to colour the work with oil colours, well thinned with turps, blending them well one with the other. It is impossible for anyone to colour a case exactly from written descriptions alone; nature must be copied if success is to be achieved. Select a piece of suitable ground, or rock, make a sketch, and reproduce it in the case. It may be necessary to chip off a piece of rock, or carefully carry home some soil, etc., and then mix the colours to match; suitable colours are:—

Soil.—Yellow, burnt sienna (with or without burnt umber), and black, making the hollow parts rather darker, and dusting on Saxon green on the higher parts.

Chalk.—Mix the sand with the glue and plaster, and do not throw on sand afterwards. First a thin wash of yellow, then in parts the faintest tinge of carmine, and a line or two with a lead pencil to mark the strata. Damp, slimy surfaces may be dark green. Varnish if intended to look wet.

Sandstone.—The colours are similar, but the points may be whitened, red sand dusted on in parts, and horizontal places made slimy.

Rough sea rocks.—These are almost black, with green edges and the faintest trace of white over all. Varnish if intended to look wet. Very suitable for white or light sea birds.

Footprints on mud.—These are sometimes dark slate colour, sunk about ¼ in. deep.

Peat.—This is often used for groundwork, especially where time is an object It can be carved into any shape, glued and nailed down, and then covered with plaster, etc., as above.

Virgin cork.—This is useful for sharp irregular rocks, and for tree trunks.

Branches.—These may be made of any shape by wrapping tow round wires, then covering all with glue and throwing on powdered lichens. But they are easiest made by nailing small branches together in various directions and concealing the junctions with glue and wadding, then covering with lichens. Oak is the best wood to use, but it must be thoroughly well dried and have plenty of turpentine, slightly coloured with green paint, put over it when fixed together. The paint improves the appearance, and the turpentine destroys small larvæ.

Ferns.—The English ferns suitable for cases are but few, the best being the common brake. This should be gathered on a dry day in autumn, pressed between sheets of newspaper or blotting-paper, and, when dry, coloured with oil paints. They look better if varied in colour; therefore colour some with light green, making the centres darker. Others can be coloured with stone colour or yellow, with brown or red centres. (These have quite faded.) Some are green, with the tips brown (beginning to fade); others are green on one side and brown on the other, and so on. They may be bent to almost any shape when the paint is dry by being carefully drawn between the finger and thumb.

Leaves.—The artificial leaves are used, but they should be the best that can be bought.

Grasses.—Any hayfield supplies a variety of grasses, which, when in seed, dry well and readily take dye; but dull colours only should be used, and most grasses, indeed, are best used uncoloured. Many coarse grasses (not the seed stalks) grow near the sea and in uncultivated places, in tufts, and most of these dry well and can be easily coloured. Hosts of the seed stalks of weeds may be collected in late autumn, and take colour nicely, but the seed must be removed first. Use oil colours for all ferns, grass, etc. The most difficult colour to imitate is the green colour of grass; but a mixture of white and chromo green should prove satisfactory. Dyes should be used only for grass in flower and for moss. Sedges and rushes dry well, and also colour well. Rushes, etc., are usually ironed to keep them from shrivelling.

Seaweeds.—These must be well washed in order to remove the salt, and should be varnished if intended to look wet. Starfish dry well (after being well washed), but should be tinted to restore the colours. These and shells, as well as all the above, are fixed sufficiently tightly with glue.

Having finished colouring the rockwork, the discoloured parts (feet, legs, cere, etc.) of the stuffed bird must be restored by painting, if not already done, all unnecessary wires, etc., removed, and the grasses, etc., fixed; and then, as a last operation, the whole bird should be covered with benzoline to destroy any insect which may be present (see also pp. 40 and 41). The benzoline will soon evaporate, and the whole should then be put into the case and fastened with two or three screws. The glass is now fixed, and strips of paper placed where required, these strips being coated afterwards with either brunswick black or japan black.

INDEX.

American Skin-preserving Method, 113
Animals (see separate headings)
Antlers (see also Horns)
——, Cleaning, 84, 85, 86
——, Mounting, as Hat-pegs, 84
——, Polishing, 84, 85, 86
Arsenical Soap, 16
Artificial Earth, etc., 154, 155
—— Eyes, 36, 37, 66, 101
Awls, Using, 14

Badger Skin, Cleaning, 115
Bamboo Uprights, Cases with, 150
Becœur's Preservative, 16
Beetles, Setting, 137
Bellhanger's Pliers, 12
Bird, Arranging Feathers of, 31, 32
——, Attitudes of, 36, 38, 39
—— Bodies of Cork and Peat, 34
—— ——, "Soft," 32
—— ——, Tow, 25
—— ——, Wire for, 36
—— Cases, 149-153
——, Cleaning, 39, 40
—— Eggs (see Eggs)
—— in Flight, 38, 39
——, Fixing, to Stand, 30
——, Inserting Artificial Eyes in, 29
——, Protecting, from Insects, 40, 41, 156
——, Placing, in Case, 153
——, Preservatives for, 16, 17
——, Removing Blood from, 39
——, Restoring Bright Colours of, 35
—— Screens, 42-47
—— Skinning, 18-23
—— Skins, Relaxing, 24
—— ——, Removing Fat from, 21
—— ——, Sewing, 28
—— Stuffing, 25-30
—— Wattles, 30
—— Webs Shrivelling, 39
——, White-fronted, Skinning, 22
—— Wiring, 25-28, 33, 34
Black Dye for Skins, 118, 119, 129
Blackbirds, Eyes for, 36
Bleaching Bones and Horns, 91-93
—— Sheepskin, 126, 127
—— Teeth, 65
Blood, Removing, from Birds, 39
Blowing Eggs, 138
Blowpipe for Eggs, 138
Blue Dye for Sheepskin, 129
Bodkin, 14

Bolting Leg Wires, 27
Bone, Removing, from Horns, 90
Bones, Bleaching, 92, 93
——, Cleaning, 92, 93
——, Fish, Preserving, 105, 106
——, ——, Varnishing, 106
——, Polishing, 93
——, Softening, 93
Book Boxes for Insects, 139
Braces for Setting Insects, 134, 135
Brain-spoon and Hook, 12
Branches, Imitating, in Cases, 155
Brown Dye for Skins, 118, 129
Browne's Preservatives, 17, 73
Brushes, Fox, Softening, 119
Buffalo Horns, Bleaching, 91
—— ——, Dyeing, 91
—— ——, Mounting, 91, 92
—— ——, Polishing, 91
Bullock Horns, Polishing, 89
—— ——, Removing Bone from 90
Butterflies, Braces for, 134, 135
——, Envelopes for, 132
——, Killing, 132
——, Pins for Fixing, 136
——, Preservative for, 141
——, Relaxing, 134
——, Setting, 134-136
——, Setting-boards for, 134
——, Tweezers for Holding, 133

Cabinets, Egg and Insect, 139-148
Case with Bamboo Uprights, 150
——, Canted Cornered, 150
——, Curved Glass, 150, 151
——, Ebonising, 151
—— for Eggs, 139-148
——, Ferns and Grasses used in, 155
——, Finishing Inside of, 152
—— for Fish, 102, 150, 151
——, Glass-ended, 149
——, Hillocks in, 153, 154
——, Artificial Branches in, 155
——, —— Chalk and Rocks in, 154
——, —— Mud Footprints in, 155
——, —— Sandstone in, 154
——, —— Soil in, 154
—— for Insects, 139-143
——, Leaves used in, 155
——, Lining, with Paper, 152
——, Painting Inside of, 152, 153
——, Peat used in, 155
——, Placing Stuffed Bird in, 153
——, Seaweed used in, 156
—— for Stuffed Specimens, 149-153

Casting Fish, 102-104
Cat, Attitude of, 65, 66
—— Skins, Treatment of, 121
——, Wires for Body of, 60
Caterpillars, Preserving, 136, 137
Chain and Hooks, 15
Chalk, Imitating, in Cases, 154
Cleaning Birds, 39, 40
—— Fish Bones, 105, 106
—— Ram's Horns, 89, 91
—— Sheep's Head, 115, 116, 125
—— Skin, 115-117, 125
—— Stag's Antlers, 84-86
—— Teeth, 65
Colouring Fish, 100, 101
Cork Body of Bird, 34
—— for Insect Cabinets, 140, 141
Corrosive Sublimate, 40, 41
Crabs, Preserving, 106
Crows, Eyes for, 36
——, Wire for Bodies of, 36
Curing (see Preserving and Skins)
Currying, 109
Cutting Nippers, 11

Davie's Corrosive Sublimate, 41
Deer's Antlers as Hat-pegs, 84
—— Head, Mounting, 68-83
Dog, Attitude of, 66
——, Feet of, 56
——, Producing Skeleton of, 92
—— Teeth, Bleaching, 65
——, Wires for Body of, 60
Duck, Attitudes of, 38
——, Eyes for, 36
——, Skinning, 23
—— Webs Shrivelling, 39
——, Wire for Body of, 36
Dye Fixative, Reimann's, 118
Dyeing Horn, 89, 91
—— Skins, 117-119, 128, 129

Eagles, Eyes for, 36
——, Wires for Bodies of, 36
Ear Blocks, 74
Eggs, Blowing, 138
——, Cabinets for, 139-148
——, Classification of, 143, 144
—— Crumbling, Preventing, 138, 139
Elephant Tusks, Mounting, 88
—— ——, Polishing, 87
Entomological Cabinets, 139-143
—— Pins, 136
Envelopes, Insect, 132
Eyes, Artificial, 29, 36, 37, 66, 101
Eye-lids, Colouring Edge of, 82

Fat, Removing, from Bird Skins, 21
——, Removing, from Skins, 113
Feathers of Bird, Arranging, 31
—— Stained by Putty, 29
Feet, Mammals', 56
Ferns used in Cases, 155
——, Painting, 155

Ferrets, Wires for Bodies of, 60
File, 15
Finches, Eyes for, 36
——, Wire for Bodies of, 36
Fire-screens, Stuffed Bird, 47
Fish, Artificial Eyes for, 101
—— Bones, Preserving, 105, 106
—— ——, Varnishing, 106
——, Cases for, 102, 150, 151
——, Casting, 102-105
——, Colouring, 100, 101
—— Fins, Treating, 99, 101
——, Flints for, 101
—— Head Shrivelling, 101, 103
——, Modelling, 102-104
——, Painting, 100, 101
——, Skeletonising, 105, 106
——, Skinning, 94-97
——, Stuffing, 98-102
——, Wire Shape of, 94, 95
Fleshing Skins, 107
Flints, 101 (see Artificial Eyes)
Folding Skins, Method of, 114
Footprints, Imitating, in Cases, 155
——, Measuring, 38
Fox Brushes, Softening, 110
—— Feet, 56
—— Tail, Skinning, 52
—— Teeth, Bleaching, 65
——, Wires for Body of, 60
Furrier's Knives, 110
—— Method of Preserving Skins, 113

Geese, Eyes for, 36
——, Skinning, 23
——, Wire for Bodies of, 36
Glass Mounts and Shades, 151
Glass-ended Cases, 149-151
Goat Skins, Cleaning, 117
—— ——, Curing, 119
—— ——, Dyeing, 117, 118
Grape Scissors, 10
Grasses used in Cases, 156
Grease in Skins, Killing, 115
Greasing Skins, 114
Green Dye for Sheepskin, 129
Grey Dye for Skins, 118, 129
Grebes, Skinning, 23
Gulls, Attitudes of, 38, 39
——, Eyes for, 36
Gull's Webs Shrivelling, 39

Hare Skins, Curing, 121
Hat-pegs, Mounting Antlers as, 84
Hawks, Eyes for, 36
—— Seizing Prey, Attitude of, 38
——, Wire for Bodies of, 36
Heads, Horned, Cleaning, 72
——, ——, Keeping Insects from, 83
——, ——, Modelling, 75-80
——, ——, Mounting, 68
——, ——, Mounts or Shields for, 81
——, ——, Preserving Skin of, 68, 73
——, ——, Skinning, 69-72.

INDEX.

Heads, Sheep, Cleaning, 116
Herons, Eyes for, 36
———, Wire for Bodies of, 36
Hillocks in Showcase, 153, 154
Hook and Brain-spoon, 12
Hooks and Chain, 15
———, Suspending, 15
Horned Heads (see Heads)
Horns (see also Antlers and names of respective Animals)
———, Bleaching, 91
———, Cleaning, 84-86, 89, 91
———, Dyeing, 89, 91
———, Mounting, 88, 89, 91, 92
———, Polishing, 84-6, 88, 89, 91
———, Removing Bone from, 90
———, Varnishing, 91
Horses, Producing Skeletons of, 92
Hunters' Treatment of Skins, 113

Insect Preventives, 40, 41, 83, 119
Insects (see also Butterflies)
———, Cabinets for, 139-143
———, Preserving, 132-137

Jack, Colouring, 100
Jays, Eyes for, 36

Killing Butterflies, etc., 132
Killing-bottles, 132
Knife for Bird Skinning, 9, 10
———, Double-edged, 110
———, Single-edged, 110
———, Skiving, 10

Leaves used in Cases, 155
Leather of Skins, Reducing, 110, 111
Leg Wires, Bolting, 27
Leopard Skin, Curing, 114, 121, 122
Lining Cases, 152

Mammals, Attitudes of, 65
———, Cleaning Teeth of, 65
——— with Open Mouths, 64
———, Preservative for, 48
———, Skinning and Stuffing, 49
———, Wiring, 62-64
Mats, Skin, 122, 125, 130
Modelling Fish, 102-104
——— Tow Body of Bird, 25
Mole, Making Purse from, 67
Monkey's Hands and Feet, 56
Moths (see Butterflies)
Mould, Plaster, for Fish, 103, 104
Mounting Antlers, 84
——— Elephant's Tusks, 87
——— Horns, 88-92
Mounts for Birds, 151
——— ——— Horned Heads, 81
Mud Footprints in Cases, 155

Nightjars, Attitudes of, 38
Nose, Animal's, Colouring, 82

Oil Removing, from Skins, 113
Otter Skin, Dressing, 130
Owls, Eyes for, 36
———, Skinning, 23
———, Wire for Bodies of, 36
Ox Horns, Polishing, 89
——— ———, Removing Bone from, 90

Paint for Brightening Colours of Bird, 35
Painting Ferns, 155
——— Fish, 100, 101
——— Insides of Cases, 152
Papier-mâché Cast of Fish, 104, 105
Park's Skin-preserving Method, 112
Partridges, Eyes for, 36
Peat, Stuffing Birds with, 34
——— used in Cases, 155
Perch, Skinning and Stuffing, 94-101
Pheasants, Eyes for, 36
Pike, Colouring, 100
Pins, Entomological, 136
Plaster Cast of Fish, 102-104
——— Modelling, 76
Plaster-of-paris, Use of, in Bird Skinning, 18
Pliers, 11-13
Plumber's Shave-hook, 108
Polishing Elephant Tusks, 87
——— Horns, 88, 89, 91
Preservative, Becœur's, 16
——— for Birds, 16, 17
———, Browne's, 17
——— for Butterflies, etc., 141
——— ——— Mammals, 48
——— ——— Skins, 108, 112-131
Preserving Caterpillars, 136, 137
——— Eggs, 138, 139
——— Insects, 132-137
——— Skins, 73, 107-131
Purse made from Mole, 67
Putty Staining Feathers, 29

Rabbit Skins, Cleaning, 118
——— ———, Curing, 111, 121-123
——— ———, Dyeing, Black, 118
——— ———, Tanning, 123
Ram's Horn, Cleaning, 89, 91
——— ———, Dyeing, 89
——— ———, Mounting, 89
——— ———, Polishing, 89, 91
——— ———, Removing Bone from, 90
——— ———, Varnishing, 91
Red Dye for Sheepskin, 129
Reimann's Dye Fixative, 118
Relaxing Bird Skins, 24
——— Insects, 134
Rhinoceros Hide, Curing, 131
Roach, Colouring, 100
Rocks, Imitating, in Cases, 155
Rugs, Skin, 122, 125, 129, 130

Scissor or Feather Pliers, 13
Scissors, 10

Screens, Bird, 42-47
Seaweed used in Cases, 156
Setting Insects, 134-137
Setting-boards, 134
Sewing Bird Skin, 28
Shades, Glass, 151
Shave-hook, 109
Sheep's Head, Cleaning, 116
Sheepskins, Bleaching, 125, 127
———, Cleaning, 115, 116, 125
———, Curing, 125, 126
———, Dyeing, 128, 129
———, Removing Wool from, 127, 128
———, Rugs made from, 125
———, Smoothing, 127
———, Softening, 130
Shields for Horned Heads, 81
Shoemaker's Awls, 14
Showcases, 102, 149-156
Side Cutters, 11
Skeletons, Producing, 92, 93, 105, 106
Skinning Birds, 18-23
——— Fish, 94-97
——— Mammals, 48-57
Skins (see also names of animals)
———, American Method of Preserving, 113
———, Cleaning, 115-117, 125
———, Disguising Smell of, 125
———, Dyeing, 118, 119, 129
———, Fleshing, 107
———, Folding, 114
———, Furrier's Method of Preserving, 113
———, Greasing, 114
——— of Horned Heads, Preserving, 68, 73
———, Hunters' Treatment of, 113
———, Killing Grease in, 115
———, Knives for Dressing, 110
———, Park's Method of Preserving, 112
———, Preservatives for, 73, 108, 112-131
———, Reducing Leather of, 110, 111
———, Removing Fat from, 113
———, ——— Oil from, 113
———, Rugs made from, 122, 125, 130
———, Russian-dressed, 120
———, Small, Preserving, 111, 121
———, Softening, 115, 119, 125, 130, 131
———, Stretching, 108
———, Tanning, 120
———, Tawing, 120
———, Tool for Scraping, 109
Skiving Knife, 10
Snake Skins, Softening, 130
Soap, Arsenical, 16
———, Browne's, 17
Soft Body Process, 32

Softening Bones, 93
——— Skins, 115, 119, 125, 130
Soil, Imitating, in Cases, 154
Squirrel, Measuring, 50
———, Skinning and Stuffing, 49
Stag's Antlers (see Antlers)
Stand, Fixing Bird to, 30
Starlings, Eyes for, 36
———, Skinning and Stuffing, 18-34
———, Wire for Bodies of, 36
Stick Handle, Mounting Horn as, 89
Sticks, Rhinoceros Hide, 131
Stoats, Wires for Bodies of, 60
Stretching-frame for Skins, 108
Stuffing Birds, 25-39
——— Fish, 98-102
——— Mammals, 57-69
——— Star Fish, 106
Stuffing-iron, 13
Swans, Skinning, 23

Tails, Bird, Setting, 32
———, Mammals, Skinning, 52
Tanning Skins, 120, 123
Tawing, 107, 120
Tendon of Achilles, 61
Thrushes, Eyes for, 36
Tiger Skin, Cleaning, 116
Tools, 9-15
Tow Body, Modelling, 25
Trout, Colouring, 101
Tweezers, Insect, 133

Varnishing Fish Bones, 106
——— Horns, 75, 91
Veined Eyes, 66

Walking-stick Handle, Mounting Ram's Horn as, 89
Walking-sticks, Rhinoceros Hide, 131
Waterbuck, Measuring, 49
Waterton's Method of Bird Stuffing, 25
Wattles, Bird, 30
Weasels, Skinning, 55
———, Wires for Bodies of, 60
Webs, Preventing, Shrivelling, 39
White Leather Dressing, 107
White-fronted Bird, Skinning, 22
Wire for Bodies of Birds, 36
——— ——— ——— Mammals, 60
——— Shape of Fish, 94, 95
Wiring Birds, 25-28, 33, 34
——— Mammals, 62-64
Wolves, Wires for Bodies of, 60
Woodpeckers, Attitudes of, 38
———, Skinning, 23
Wool, Removing, from Skins, 127, 128

Yellow Dye for Sheepskin, 129